ORIGINAL TEXT, ENGLISH TRANSLATION,
AND A COMMENTARY ON AMAND VANDERHAGEN'S
*MÉTHODE NOUVELLE ET RAISONNÉE
POUR LA CLARINETTE* (1785) AND *NOUVELLE MÉTHODE
DE CLARINETTE* (1799)

A Study in Eighteenth-Century French Clarinet Music

ORIGINAL TEXT, ENGLISH TRANSLATION,
AND A COMMENTARY ON AMAND VANDERHAGEN'S
*MÉTHODE NOUVELLE ET RAISONNÉE
POUR LA CLARINETTE* (1785) AND *NOUVELLE MÉTHODE
DE CLARINETTE* (1799)

A Study in Eighteenth-Century French Clarinet Music

Joan Michelle Blazich

With a Foreword by
David Ross

The Edwin Mellen Press
Lewiston•Queenston•Lampeter

Library of Congress Cataloging-in-Publication Data

Blazich, Joan Michelle.
  Original text, English translation, and a commentary on Amand Vanderhagen's Methode nouvelle et raisonnee pour la clarinette (1785) and Nouvelle methode de clarinette (1799) : a study in eighteenth-century French clarinet music / Joan Michelle Blazich ; with a foreword by David Ross.
     p. cm.
  "Vanderhagen's Ouvre [sic]": p.
  Includes bibliographical references and index.
  ISBN-13: 978-0-7734-4686-1
  ISBN-10: 0-7734-4686-9
  1. Clarinet--Methods. 2. Vanderhagen, Amand, 1753-1822. Mithode nouvelle et raisonnie pour la clarinette. 3. Vanderhagen, Amand, 1753-1822. Nouvelle mithode de clarinette. I. Vanderhagen, Amand, 1753-1822. Mithode nouvelle et raisonnie pour la clarinette. English. II. Vanderhagen, Amand, 1753-1822. Nouvelle mithode de clarinette. English. III. Title.
  MT382.B599 2009
  788.6'2193--dc22
                                    2009026543

hors série.

A CIP catalog record for this book is available from the British Library.

Front cover photo: *Gamme Naturelle* courtesy of Bibliothèque nationale de France

Copyright © 2009 Joan Michelle Blazich

All rights reserved. For information contact

> The Edwin Mellen Press   The Edwin Mellen Press
> Box 450   Box 67
> Lewiston, New York   Queenston, Ontario
> USA 14092-0450   CANADA L0S 1L0

> The Edwin Mellen Press, Ltd.
> Lampeter, Ceredigion, Wales
> UNITED KINGDOM SA48 8LT

Printed in the United States of America

In loving memory of Joan Maxine Wooden

Table of Contents

Foreword by David Ross — i

Acknowledgements — v

Illustrations — vii

Introduction — 1

Chapter 1 — 5
Amand Vanderhagen

Chapter 2 — 29
Méthode nouvelle et raisonnée pour la clarinette (1785)

Chapter 3 — 93
Nouvelle méthode de clarinette (1799)

Chapter 4 — 213
A Commentary on *Méthode nouvelle et raisonnée pour la clarinette* and *Nouvelle méthode de clarinette*

Chapter 5 — 233
The Relationship Between the Treatises of Vanderhagen, Blasius, and Lefèvre

Chapter 6 — 247
The Legacy of Amand Vanderhagen

Appendix One — 249
Vanderhagen's Œuvre

Appendix Two — 259
Works by Amand Vanderhagen Currently In Print

Appendix Three — 261
Listing of Content for the Methods of Vanderhagen, Blasius, and Lefèvre

Bibliography — 265

Index — 271

Foreword

It is with much pleasure that I write this foreword to Joan Blazich's study of Amand Vanderhagen, for it underscores my own interest in attempting to connect the performance traditions and the playing personalities of earlier generations of clarinetists with those of today. For most musicians, this "reaching back" into playing traditions and roots extends only a short distance, to what our immediate teachers have told us and perhaps, via recordings or writings, to some important players of the preceding generation, our "grandteachers" as it were. But of course all of us are products of a much longer performance tradition, extending back over the centuries to players and teaching personalities who, though perhaps only names to us today, exerted an important influence on their contemporaries, an influence which extends in subtle and not so subtle ways to our present day.

While Amand Vanderhagen is a name not unknown to students of clarinet history, this is the first study which fleshes out in any great detail his life and work, as well as presenting an English translation with commentary on his two clarinet methods written for the Classical five-keyed clarinet. Both the *Méthode nouvelle et raisonnée pour la clarinette* from 1785 and the *Nouvelle méthode de clarinette* of 1799 are significant in a number of ways. Foremost is the fact that the earlier method is the first pedagogical work devoted solely to the clarinet, and as such it provided a model for later clarinet instruction books, at least those originating from France. Earlier instructional materials such as Roeser's *Essai d'instruction* (1764) and the article on the "Clarinette" in the *Supplément à l'Encyclopedie* (1776) do mention the clarinet, but more in a descriptive fashion and in theoretical/compositional terms, giving composers and musicians an idea of what the clarinet was capable of and how one could use it. By way of contrast,

Vanderhagen includes more pedagogical instructions specific to the clarinet, concepts such as forming an embouchure, holding the instrument, choosing reeds, and articulation syllables.

As Blazich points out, these Vanderhagen methods probably served as a "template" for later French clarinet methods, including the influential *Méthode de clarinette* from 1802 by Jean Xavier Lefèvre, which was adopted as the "official" clarinet method by the newly founded Paris Conservatory and remained in print and in use well into the twentieth century. Thus in a very direct way Vanderhagen played a role in the formation of a French school of clarinet playing, and more obliquely, in the standardization of training and performance brought about by the establishment of national conservatories, of which Paris was the first example. The fact that during this period the clarinet was being more widely accepted and used as a "first" instrument on which one could learn music is demonstrated by the differences between Vanderhagen's first treatise of 1785 and his second some fourteen years later. The first deals primarily with problems directly related to playing the clarinet, working from the assumption that the student already knew the rudiments of music and indeed probably played another instrument before starting the clarinet. The latter work does not make this assumption, beginning at a lower level of musical knowledge and including lengthy sections on fundamentals and the reading of music. Clearly this difference is reflective of social changes, both in the type (and perhaps numbers) of students taking up the clarinet and also of a more general acceptance of the clarinet into the musical world.

As one might expect from a pedagogical work originating from the end of the eighteenth century, some of the concepts presented here are clearly outmoded. Probably most obvious is the idea of playing with the reed on the topside of the mouthpiece, a practice that was still employed by French clarinetists until slightly after Vanderhagen's death in 1822. But many of his suggestions, ideas, and thoughts about clarinet playing have as much relevance today as they did in his own lifetime. His description on holding the instrument along with finger placement/action sounds quite modern, as do his comments about reed quality and strength. His complaint about students wishing only to play what is popular without learning new material can certainly be echoed by many of today's teachers. And his use of varying syllables for different articulations has a parallel in modern teaching. While neither of these methods can be used directly as clarinet tutors today, a careful reading of Vanderhagen's materials reveals much which can be utilized by modern instrument players as well as by period instrument specialists.

David Ross

David Ross is a clarinetist, musicologist, and one of today's leading scholars on the history of the clarinet. He is Professor of Music at the University of Texas at El Paso.

Acknowledgements

I would like to especially thank bruce d. mcclung for his tireless help and support of this project, from answering countless questions to editing seemingly endless drafts. Many thanks also to Lowanne Jones, Steven Cohen, Christine Getz, Albert Rice, Ingrid Pearson, and Jesse Krebs for their kindness and effort in editing, answering questions, and offering suggestions. Special thanks are owed to David Ross for his lovely foreword. I am also grateful to the Bibliothèque nationale de France for granting copyright permission for selected images from Vanderhagen's methods that were not transcribable by modern methods. Finally, I would like to thank my parents and my brother for their continued support of my work, as well as my late grandmother, whose excitement over this book has not been diminished by her untimely passing. Merci!

Illustrations

The images on the following pages are reproduced with the kind permission of the Bibliothèque nationale de France (BnF): *Methode nouvelle et raisonnee pour la clarinette* (1785) title page, The Natural Scale, and Scale of Sharps and Flats; *Nouvelle methode de clarinette* (1799) title page, The Natural Scale, Scale on the Sharps and Flats, and Article Two: Of the Value and Shape of Notes. All other images are modern transcriptions by the author.

Introduction

Although Amand Vanderhagen (1753–1822) is periodically cited as a clarinetist and author of pedagogical treatises, his contributions to the development and advancement of the instrument have yet to be fully recognized. As the author of the first two known published methods on the Classical clarinet, *Méthode nouvelle et raisonnée pour la clarinette* (1785) and *Nouvelle méthode de clarinette* (1799), Vanderhagen revolutionized musical instruction, particularly as regards clarinetists. With these works Vanderhagen establishes the foundation for the concept of the modern clarinet method book, from fingering charts and descriptions of the embouchure to music fundamentals and etudes. Vanderhagen's writings reflect the performance practices of his time, and each treatise still offers thorough explanations of technique that are remarkably similar to many modern methods, evincing Vanderhagen's importance in advancing clarinet pedagogy from the Baroque to the Classical eras, and beyond.

The Baroque clarinet, which existed from ca. 1700–1780s, was an instrument of two or three keys, with a limited range and usability.[1] Treatises for this instrument often consisted of little more than rudimentary fingering charts and a few sentences of advice. The lengthiest Baroque treatise on the clarinet, Valentin Roeser's *Essai d'instruction à l'usage de ceux qui composent pour la clarinette et la cor* (1764), contains several paragraphs regarding the range and capabilities of the four-keyed clarinet,[2] but offers no specific information on clarinet pedagogy.

---

[1] Albert Rice, *The Baroque Clarinet* (Oxford: Clarendon Press, 1992), 64–78.

[2] Ibid., 135–36.

In contrast, by the 1770s the clarinet was an instrument of five or six keys, capable of playing in all genres and styles.³ By the beginning of the nineteenth century, clarinet treatises, from Jean-Xavier Lefèvre's *Méthode de clarinette à 13 clefs* (1802) to Ivan Müller's *Méthode pour la nouvelle clarinette et clarinette-alto* (c. 1821), offered substantial discussions of all aspects of the clarinet.⁴ The majority of all Classical clarinet treatises, however, are based on those of Vanderhagen, particularly with regard to his descriptions of body posture, embouchure, and articulation. His pedagogy can be regarded as extremely advanced for the time because Vanderhagen, unlike prior authors, gives specific, detailed instructions on how to hold the instrument, breathe properly, create the embouchure, and choose appropriate reeds. Vanderhagen's descriptions of using syllables for certain articulations, as well as his advice on playing with the reed above, are the most substantive writings on these subjects to date. Although Vanderhagen's advice to play with the reed on the top of the mouthpiece is no longer practiced, the rest of his instructions prefigure contemporary pedagogy. Despite the occasional acknowledgement of Vanderhagen's contributions to clarinet instruction and its subsequent influences on other clarinetists, there have been no available translations of either of Vanderhagen's treatises until now.

This study offers, for the first time, a substantial and well-researched examination of Vanderhagen's life and accomplishments, and full English translations of both treatises. Although Vanderhagen uses both terms and concepts that are now considered archaic, the translations seek to preserve his original writings as much as possible. The availability of these English translations should prove to be of enormous benefit to our understanding of the early Classical clarinet and of the nascent development of clarinet pedagogy. In addition, this study should provide Vanderhagen with the long-awaited

---

³ Extant instruments indicate that five-key clarinets were made in London by 1770, with Parisian instrument makers adopting the London makers' five-keyed system by late the 1770s.

⁴ Rice, *The Clarinet in the Classical Period* (Oxford: Oxford University Press, 2003), 66.

recognition he deserves as the "founder of the method book for clarinet." Although others soon overshadowed his methods, Vanderhagen's treatises provided subsequent clarinetists with the inspiration and organizational template upon which to base their own methods.

Finally, Vanderhagen's two treatises have been analyzed and compared to two contemporary works, Frédéric Blasius's *Nouvelle méthode de clarinette* (1796) and Jean Xavier Lefèvre's *Méthode de clarinette* (1802). These comparisons show how modern Vanderhagen's teachings were for that era and the impression his work made on his colleagues. The influence of Vanderhagen's methods on his immediate contemporaries is demonstrated through a close comparison of their treatises, which reveals paraphrasing and outright lifting of specific passages.

Although Vanderhagen wrote an additional treatise for the clarinet, *Nouvelle méthode pour la clarinette moderne à douze clefs* (1819), this treatise will not been addressed here because it concerns the twelve-keyed clarinet, an instrument significantly more advanced than the five-keyed clarinet described in his *Méthode nouvelle et raisonnée pour la clarinette*. I have also not addressed any additional treatises beyond those of Blasius and Lefèvre because these are the most significant Classical treatises for the clarinet from this time period. The immense popularity of the treatises by Vanderhagen, Blasius, and Lefèvre confirms that these four works should be compared because they present the most complete body of information on the Classical clarinet between 1785–1802.

Chapter 1
Amand Vanderhagen

A Brief History of the Clarinet to 1785

Most historians credit the invention of the clarinet, c.1700, to Johann Christoph Denner (1655–1707), a German instrument maker. The first reference to the creation of this new instrument occurs in J. G. Doppelmayr's *Historische Nachricht von den Nürnbergischen Mathematicis und Kunstlern* (1730): "At the beginning of the present century he [Denner] invented a new sort of pipe, the so-called *Clarinette*, to the great satisfaction of music-lovers, and at length presented an improved chalumeau."[5] Denner's first clarinets, now known as two-keyed clarinets, had separate mouthpieces, two body joints, two keys for A^4 and B^4, and the range of a twelfth. The chalumeau, in contrast, consisted of a two-piece body that had a limited range of a tenth.[6] Doppelmayr's statement on the invention of the clarinet has raised questions over whether the clarinet was truly invented or the result of an improved chalumeau, although current research indicates that the clarinet and the chalumeau are two separate instruments.

The rising popularity and greater flexibility of the clarinet eventually led to the abandonment of the chalumeau. Some pieces originally composed for chalumeau were republished for clarinet, while other works could be played on either instrument, such as *Airs à deux Chalumeaux ou deux Clarinettes* (1716) by

---

[5] J. G. Doppelmayr, *Historische Nachricht von den Nürnbergischen Mathematicis und Künstlern* (1730), trans. F. G. Rendall in *The Clarinet: Some Notes Upon Its History and Construction*, 3rd ed. (New York: W. W. Norton and Company, 1971), 65.

[6] Colin Lawson, "Chalumeau." *Grove Music Online. Oxford Music Online.* 7 December 2008. <http://www.oxfordmusiconline.com/subscriber/article/grove/music/05376>.

an anonymous composer.[7] Orchestral, operatic, and chamber music for both the chalumeau and two-keyed clarinet consisted mostly of doubling trumpet parts because they had bright, piercing timbres. J. Mattheson, in *Das neu-eröffnete Orchester* (1713), claimed, "The so-called chalumeaux may be allowed to voice their somewhat howling symphony on an evening, perhaps in June or July and from a distance, but never in January at a serenade on the water."[8] The clarinet was not considered favorably either, as J. E. Altenburg, in *Versuch einer Anleitung zur heroisch-musikalischen Trompeter und Pauker-Kunst* (1795), observed, "The strident piercing sound of this instrument is most useful in the military music of the infantry, and it sounds much better from afar than close to."[9]

By the 1730s instrument makers were refining the clarinet to produce purer tones. The relocation of the register key towards the mouthpiece and a reduction in the size of its vent hole allowed for the production of Bb^4. The improvement of Bb^4 resulted in the loss of B^4, although instrument makers corrected this problem by lengthening the bottom joint, boring a new hole for B^4, and adding a bell for additional resonance. A long shank and key mechanism connected to the new hole allowed for the venting of a proper B^4 and extended the range of the clarinet from low F^3 to E^3. The lengthening of the instrument also increased the number of joints from four to five or six, including the mouthpiece, barrel, left-hand joint, right-hand joint, lower joint, and bell. The lower joint and bell were initially joined, creating what is now termed a stock-bell.[10] The three-keyed clarinet, developed by 1740, is generally termed "the Baroque clarinet"

---

[7] *Airs à deux Chalumeau ou deux Clarinettes* (Amsterdam: Roger et Le Cène, 1716).

[8] J. Mattheson, *Das neu-eröffnete Orchester* (1713), trans. Oscar Kroll in *The Clarinet*, trans. Hilda Morris, ed. Anthony Baines (New York: Taplinger Publishing Company, 1968), 15.

[9] J. E. Altenburg, *Versuch einer Anleitung zur heroisch-musikalischen Trompeter und Pauker-Kunst* ([ca. 1770] n.p., 1795), trans. Oscar Kroll in *The Clarinet*, 23–24.

[10] Rice, *The Clarinet in the Classical Period*, 13.

because several late Baroque composers, including Vivaldi and Handel, composed for it.[11]

The addition of keys for low $F\#^3$ and $G\#^3$ during the middle of the eighteenth century resulted in the five-keyed clarinet being produced by 1770. By 1790 the addition of a sixth key for middle $C\#^4$ made the "five-keyed clarinet" capable of spanning an almost four-octave range. Instrument makers also produced clarinets at various pitch levels to accommodate works composed in particular keys. Treatises and surviving instruments indicate that clarinets were pitched in G, A, Bb, B, C, D, Eb, E, and F, although the most common keys were C, Bb, and A.[12] The production of variously pitched instruments allowed the clarinet to be used in almost every musical situation, and its flexibility made it extremely popular with Classical composers and players as witnessed by the number of extant compositions and instruments.[13]

Instructional Treatises on the Clarinet c. 1732–1785

Clarinet treatises appeared sporadically during the eighteenth century. The first known publication that provides any type of instructional material on the clarinet is Joseph Friedrich Majer's *Museum Musicum theoretico practicum das ist neu-eröffneter theoretische und practischer Music-Saal* (1732). Majer provides a brief description of the clarinet and gives a fingering chart for a two-keyed clarinet:

> The clarinet is a wooden wind instrument invented by a man from Nürnberg at the beginning of this century, and is not unlike a long oboe, except that it has a broad mouthpiece. The sound of this instrument from

---

[11] Rendall, 73–75.

[12] Rice, 21–22.

[13] Ibid., 72.

afar is not unlike that of the trumpet and has a range from the tenor f to the second a^5 and sometimes to the third c^6.[14]

A second edition of Majer's *Museum Musicum* published in 1741 simply reprints the information on the clarinet given in his 1732 edition, despite the existence of three-keyed instruments by this time. Another contemporary reference to the early (two- or three-keyed) clarinet occurs in Johann Philipp Eisel's *Musicus Autodidaktos, oder der sich selbst informirende musicus* (1738), although Eisel bases his information on that of Majer.[15]

The three-keyed clarinet continued to be used into the late eighteenth and early nineteenth centuries as witnessed by two later publications. Lorents Nicolai Berg, in his Norwegian instrumentation treatise *Den første prove for begyndere udi instrumental-kunsten* (1782), provides a fingering chart for the three-keyed clarinet but states in the text that the usual clarinet has five keys.[16] The second source is a single handwritten fingering chart for the three-keyed clarinet (with an E/B key for the left hand little finger), entitled *Gamut for the Clarionet*, pasted onto the flyleaf of *The Compleat Tutor for the German Flute* (1810).[17] Despite these references the three-keyed clarinet was becoming obsolete by the 1740s.

Valentin Roeser published *Essai d'instruction à l'usage de ceux qui composent pour la clarinette et le cor* (1764), the earliest treatise on the Classical clarinet, which contains several paragraphs regarding the range and abilities of the four-keyed clarinet.[18] Roeser's observation that "many sixteenth notes in succession are not employed by the clarinet, considering that the breath must

---

[14] Joseph Friedrich Majer, *Museum Musicum theoretico practicum das ist neu-eröffneter theoretisch und practischer Music-Saal* (1732), 16, quoted in Eugene Rousseau, "Clarinet Instructional Materials from 1732 to ca.1825" (Ph.D. diss., University of Iowa, 1962), 12–13.

[15] Johann Philipp Eisel, *Musicus Autodidaktos, oder der sich selbst informirende musicus* (1738) (Erfurt, Germany: J. M. Funck, 1738).

[16] Rice, 212.

[17] *The Compleat Tutor for the German Flute* (Dublin: J. Delawney, 1810).

[18] Rice, 135–36.

substitute for the tongue because the position of the reed is beneath the roof of the mouth" is the earliest known description of articulation and indicates that at this time the clarinet was played with the reed on top of the mouthpiece.[19] However, Roeser was writing for composers, not performers, and did not provide any specific information for learning how to the play the clarinet, such as descriptions of how to form an embouchure, establish correct body posture, or breathe properly.

Other treatises that discuss the four-keyed clarinet include Jacques Hotteterre's *Méthode pour apprendre à jouer en trés peu de tems de la flûte traversière et des tablatures de la clarinette* (1765),[20] Louis Joseph Francœur's *Diapason général de tous les instruments à vent* (1772),[21] Frédéric Adolphe Maximilian Gustav de Castillon in the *Supplément à L'Encyclopédie* (1776–77),[22] Abraham's *Principes de Clarinette Suivis de Pas rèdoubles et de 7 Marches les Plus a la Mode*,[23] Michel Corrette's *Méthode Raisonnée pour apprendre aisément à joüer de la Flûtte traversiere Nouvelle édition, revûe corigée et augmentée de la Gamme du Haut-bois et de la Clarinette*,[24] and *Principes de Clarinette Avec la Tablature des Meilleurs M^{tres} pour cet Instrument et plusier Duo pour cet*

---

[19] Valentin Roeser, *Essai d'instruction à l'usage de ceux qui composent pour la clarinette et le cor* (1764), 12, quoted in ibid., 130.

[20] Jacques Hotteterre, *Méthode pour apprendre à jouer en trés peu de tems de la flûte traversière et des tablatures de la clarinette* (Paris: Bailleux, 1765).

[21] Rousseau, 17–19.

[22] Frédéric Adolphe Maximilian Gustav de Castillon, "Clarinette," *Supplément à l'Encyclopédie, ou Dictionnaire Raisonné des Sciences, des Arts et des Métiers*, vol. II (Amsterdam: M. M. Rey, 1776–77), 450–51.

[23] Abraham, *Principes de Clarinette Suivis de Pas rèdoubles et de 7 Marches les Plus a la Mode* (Paris: Frere, c. 1782).

[24] Michel Corrette, *Méthode Raisonnée pour apprendre aisément à joüer de la Flûtte traversiere Nouvelle édition, revûe corigée et augmentée de la Gamme du Haut-bois et de la Clarinette* (Paris: Aux Adresses ordinares de Musique, c. 1773).

Instrument by an anonymous author.[25] Hotteterre, Castillon, Abraham, Corrette, and the *Principes de Clarinette* provide fingering charts for the four-keyed clarinet, although Hotteterre provides the only illustration of the instrument.[26] Francoeur offers substantially more information on the clarinet for composers by discussing range, tone, ornamentation, and transposition.[27] The number of sources relating to the four-keyed clarinet is remarkable considering how quickly it developed into a five-keyed instrument. Although five-keyed clarinets were being produced in London by the 1770s, the first significant treatise on the five-keyed clarinet, Amand Vanderhagen's *Méthode nouvelle et raisonnée pour la clarinette*, was not published until 1785.

Amand Vanderhagen

The son of a local organist, Amand Jean François Joseph Vanderhagen was born in 1753 in Anvers, Belgium to parents of Germanic heritage.[28] At the age of six he joined the cathedral choir of the *La cathédrale Notre-Dame d'Anvers* where his father worked.[29] After his voice broke, Vanderhagen was sent to Brussels to study music with his uncle, A. Vanderhagen, principal oboist for Prince Charles Alexander of Lorraine (1712–1780), a military commander whose marriage to Maria Anna of Hapsburg in 1744 made him Governor of the Austrian Netherlands. His palace, built in Brussels in 1757, quickly became well known for its excellent orchestra and chapel choir. While studying in Brussels, Vanderhagen

---

[25] *Principes de Clarinette Avec la Tablature des Meilleurs M^{res} pour cet Instrument et plusier Duo pour cet Instrument* (Paris: n.p., c. 1775).

[26] Ibid.

[27] Ibid.,18–19.

[28] François Joseph Fétis, *Biographie Universelle des Musiciens et Bibliographie Générale de la Musique*, vol. 8 (Paris: Chez Alph. Royer, 1844), 431.

[29] The Cathedral of Our Lady, or Onze Lieve Vrouwe Kathedraal, begun in 1352, remains the largest Gothic cathedral in Belgium and the Netherlands.

also took composition lessons from another band member, Pierre van Maldere (1729-1768).[30]

An extremely popular and prolific Belgian composer and violinist, Maldere's output reflects the early Classical style. While his chamber works represent the late Baroque era, particularly styled after Corelli, his violin sonatas and symphonies follow the characteristics of the early Viennese symphony. Maldere's symphonies are especially notable for their form, containing clear thematic contrast and modulatory developments. The second movement is typically in binary form while the third is a rondo, with the majority of his symphonies containing four movements. He served as principal violinist for Prince Charles from 1749 until his death in 1768, and in 1758 was appointed as *valet de chambre* to the Prince. Maldere also served as a court composer and conductor. In addition to his symphonies and violin sonatas, Maldere composed over forty operas, which were performed across Europe. Although seldom performed today, Maldere's works were widely recognized during his time by such contemporaries as F. J. Haydn and W. A. Mozart.[31]

Based on membership records of the *Grand Orient de France*, a Masonic organization, it can be determined that Vanderhagen moved to Paris sometime before or during 1775 and joined the band of the *Garde Françoise du Roi*.[32] A print advertisement from 1776 by a music publisher for one of his compositions further supports these Masonic records.[33] Vanderhagen's immigration date of

---

[30] Maldere's name has several known variant spellings, including Malder, van Maltre, Van Maltere, van Maldern, Wan Maldere, and wan Malder.

[31] Suzanne Clercx-Lejeune. "Maldere, Pierre van." *Grove Music Online. Oxford Music Online.*   7   December   2008. <http://www.oxfordmusiconline.com/subscriber/article/grove/music/17534>.

[32] "VANDERHAGEN [Amand] (Jean-François-Joseph) (1753-1822). *Musicien aux Gardes françaises, de 1775 à 1789.* – Le Patriotisme (Officer du Grand Orient de la Cour), 1782-88" (Alain Le Bihan, *Francs-Maçons Parisiens du Grand Orient de France* (Paris. Bibliothèque nationale, 1966), 470).

[33] 1ème Suite d'*Amusemens militaries* en harmonie pour 2 cors, 2 clarinettes & 2 bassons, contenant les airs de *la Colonie* & autres, mis en ordre par le sieur Armand VANDERAGEN,

1775 to Paris has been disputed because of records indicating that a bassoonist by the name of Vanderhagen served in this band from 1776–1785.[34] This bassoonist was too old to be Amand Vanderhagen however.

The *Grand Orient de France*, which was established in France in 1733, remains the only Masonic order in France and one of the largest in Europe. Its membership has welcomed numerous musicians, including Vanderhagen's fellow guardsmen and his professional colleagues Blasius[35] and Yost.[36] As a member of *Le Patriotisme*, a Parisian chapter sympathetic to the French royalty, Vanderhagen served as an officer for the group from 1782–88. *Le Patriotisme* disbanded in 1788 because of growing unrest in advance of the Revolution, and upon its reestablishment in 1805 Vanderhagen did not resume his membership. Although it may never be known what Vanderhagen's exact political leanings were, his membership in *Le Patriotisme* strongly hints that he was a monarchist. This political allegiance to the crown may help to explain why Vanderhagen remained in the *Garde Françoise du Roi* for much of his career. It may also explain why Blasius was able to secure a more prominent teaching position at the *Conservatoire de Paris* over him. Blasius held memberships in *Les Amis Réunis*, *Sainte-Cécile*, and *La Société Olympique*, Masonic chapters that were supportive of Revolutionary ideals. This general lack of sympathy amongst his fellow musicians towards *l'Ancien Regime* may have hurt Vanderhagen professionally, as the *Conservatoire* was developed and instituted by Revolutionaries.

---

musicien du Roi. Prix 6 liv. On donnera la suite de ces airs & on les fera tenir port franc par la poste. Chez le sieur de La Chevardière, rue du Roule (*Announces, affiches et avis divers* 7 March 1776 (supplement, p. 212)).

[34] Fetis lists Vanderhagen's emigration date to Paris as 1783 while Pamela Weston gives it as 1785. (Pamela Weston, *More Clarinet Virtuosi of the Past* (London: Halston and Co., Ltd., 1977), 262).

[35] "BLASIUS le jeune (Mathieu-Frédéric) (v. 1758–1829). *Professeur de musique*. – Les Amis Réunis, 1771–84. Sainte–Cécile, 1784. «La Société Olympique», 1786" (Le Bihan, 77).

[36] "YOST (Michel) (1754–1786). *Professeur de musique*. – Sainte-Cécile, 1784" (Le Bihan, 488).

13

At this time military bands were small ensembles, typically consisting of two to four oboes, clarinets, horns, and bassoons. These musicians were seldom listed on official military rolls, receiving payment for their services from their colonel or through officer contributions. An ordinance from April 28, 1763 indicates that each musician earned nine hundred livres per year, in addition to one hundred sixty-six livres for uniforms, instrument maintenance, and heating expenses. By 1774 the band of the French guard had been enlarged to twenty-one musicians, ten of them clarinets. Beginning around 1780 this band, along with the military band of the Swiss Guard, began to play evening concerts on the terrace at Versailles and around Paris, establishing what would quickly became a popular form of public entertainment.[37]

By 1785 Vanderhagen had become principal clarinet "and became favorably known for the marches that he composed for this ensemble."[38] Although French military bands had begun to enlarge their ensemble size by this time, they often split into smaller groups for performances, particularly quartets or sextets of winds (oboe, clarinet, or bassoon) and horns. Their music at this time consisted of marches and arrangements of opera melodies and other popular tunes. In 1789 the military, faced with severe financial strain, issued regulations stating that bands should contain between eight to ten musicians. These orders appear to have been ignored though, as by 1790 most bands contained forty-five members.[39] This continual disregard for regulations, coupled with a steady growth in band sizes, probably reflected the need for larger ensembles to participate in increasing numbers of public and patriotic displays.

---

[37] Roger Nourrison, "Regiment des Gardes Suisses 1616–1792," *Band International* 24 (2002), 23–26.

[38] "Il entra comme première clarinette dans la musique des gardes françaises, et se fit connaître avantageusement par quelques marches qu'il composa pour ce corps." (Fétis, 431).

[39] Nourrison, 24–25.

In 1788 the French Guards officially enlarged their band from sixteen to twenty-four musicians[40] and Vanderhagen became bandmaster of the group through the patronage of the Prince de Guémené.[41] The Prince of Guémené, Jules Hercule Meriadec de Rohan (1726–1800), was a close friend of Queen Marie Antoinette and a passionate lover of the arts. His patronage of Vanderhagen and this band indicates that Vanderhagen was, in some capacity, acquainted with the uppermost circle of nobility and royalty in France at this time. Vanderhagen's presence and stature in Paris is further supported by a catalogue of all known musicians in Paris from 1785 that includes him:

> Vanderhagen has made several collections of melodies chosen for the clarinet, drawn from the best of the comic operas, for quartets, duo, etc.; he is also publisher of the *Journal of Military Music* for two clarinets, two hunting horns, and two bassoons.[42]

Although copies of the *Journal of Military Music* are now considered lost, it appears from Fetis's description that it focused exclusively on music for the French military band. This sextet arrangement of two clarinets, two horns, and two bassoons served as the favored, standard French military band for much of the eighteenth century, being gradually replaced by larger bands because of an immediate need for a more audibly-present ensemble. Despite becoming obsolete in the military, this particular kind of sextet remained popular among composers and chamber music enthusiasts because of its unique timbre.

The French Revolution, which began in 1789, caused enormous turmoil and bloodshed in and around Paris. Despite the loss of many documents from this

---

[40] David Paul Swanzy, "The Wind Ensemble and Its Music During the French Revolution (1789–1795)" (Ph.D. diss., Michigan State University, 1966), 43.

[41] "Trois ans après, la protection du prince de Guémené lui fit obtenir le grade de chef de cette musique" (Fétis, 431).

[42] "*Vanderhagen*, a fait plusieurs recueils d'airs choisis pour la clarinettte, tires des meilleurs Opéra-Comiques, quatuor, duo, &c & eft Editeur du Journal d'harmonie militaire pour deux clarinettes, deux cors de chasse & deux bassons" (*Tablettes de Renommée des Musiciens* (1785); reprint, Geneva: Minkoff Reprints, 1971, n.p.).

period due to widespread unrest, looting, and burning of many government and church buildings, references to Vanderhagen periodically surface. A catalogue of Parisian musicians mentions Vanderhagen as a witness to a fellow Guard member's wedding:

> Jadin, Paul Adrien, musician of the king's guards; residing at Conti 1790, 9 June: The first son of François J. and Marie Marguerite Raisser, he has married Marie Antoinette Montauger, a youngest daughter. Witnesses: Amand Van der Hagen, residing at *rue Saint Marguerite*, in the parish of Saint Sulpice—a musician.[43]

This mention of Vanderhagen is particularly valuable because it provides, for the first time, information regarding where he lived in Paris. Although the *rue Saint Marguerite* was demolished during Baron Haussmann's street improvements during the 1850s, it is known from maps of Paris c. 1790 that Vanderhagen lived in close proximity to the *eglise Saint Sulpice*.[44] It is probable that Vanderhagen visited this church on a regular basis because of its proximity to his home, but due to its burning during the Paris Commune of 1871 any records that might have contained information regarding him are now lost.

A second mention of Vanderhagen during this time period occurs in a *carte de sûreté* from 1793.[45] *Cartes de sûreté* were security cards issued to all residents of Paris during The Terror and served as identification cards or *livrets* (worker's passbooks). This *sûreté* lists Vanderhagen as a single male, forty-eight years of age, with an occupation of musician. Based on his baptism records from 1753, he would have been forty years old in 1793. Reasons for this eight-year

---

[43] "Jadin (Paul Adrien), musicien des gardes du corps du roi; demeurant place Conti. 1790, 9 juin: Fils majeur de François J. et de Marie Marguerite Raisser. Mariage avec Marie Antoinette Montauger, fille mineure. Témoin: Amand Van der Hagen, demeurant rue Ste Marguerite, paroisse Saint Sulpice...un musicien" (Yolande de Brossard, *Musiciens de Paris 1535–1792* (Paris: Editions A. and J. Picard, 1965), 153, 279).

[44] The *eglise Saint Sulpice* was built in 1624 and by the late 1700s had become one of the most frequented churches in Paris, attracting worshippers from peasants to nobility. It is located in the area of Paris known today as the Sixième Arondissement.

[45] Bibliothéque Genealogique de Paris, *Cartes de sûreté 1792–95*, F7/4808, No. 62.

disparity between his baptismal record and *sûreté* are unknown, although his age may have been simply recorded incorrectly on the latter document. Another possibility could be that Vanderhagen may have lied about his age in order to both gain employment and receive faster promotions in the *Garde*.

Vanderhagen's *sûreté* also provides more information regarding where he lived in both Belgium and Paris. He gives his Belgium town of origin as Enverce, a small town on the outskirts of Antwerp that was eventually swallowed by Antwerp's sprawl.[46] In Paris Vanderhagen gives his specific street address as *rue Saint Marguerite 165*, with a previous address of Versailles. As a member of the *Garde Françoise du Roi* Vanderhagen was considered part of the *Maison du Roi*. This meant that Vanderhagen and his fellow musicians resided at Versailles and functioned as part of the royal staff, providing musical entertainment as requested.

The initial stages of the French Revolution were an unsettling time for the musicians of the *Garde Nationale* as bands were continuously and randomly disorganized, then reformed, because of their connection to the former monarchy.[47] This turmoil did not last long however, as many French Revolutionaries began to view music as a powerful vehicle for political and social propaganda. Large wind bands and orchestras were often quickly created to provide the French public with "acceptable" entertainment. By 1791 the band of the *Garde Nationale* was performing on a voluntary basis without pay, and on October 14, 1791 was abruptly dissolved. Dissent over the loss of this ensemble and its contributions to patriotic events quickly led to the reinstatement of the band at the urging of Bernard Sarrette and several other prominent Parisian politicians. On June 8, 1792, Sarrette invited Vanderhagen, along with the other forty-four musicians of the *Garde Nationale*, to form the *l'école de musique de la Garde Nationale*. This school was created to provide musical instruction to the numerous musicians required by the Republic's fourteen armies, but was not

---

[46] Bibliothéque Genealogique de Paris, *Cartes de sûreté 1792–95*, F7/4808, No. 62.

[47] Nourrison, 25.

officially recognized as a government institution until 1793 when Sarrette petitioned for it to become the *Institut Nationale de Musique*.[48] In 1795, after the end of The Terror, the *Institut* became a more disciplined and permanent school for music, known as the *Conservatoire de Paris*.[49]

Records from the initial years of these two music schools are unfortunately scarce, with the majority of them destroyed by fires set during the Commune of 1871. Although no records survive listing Vanderhagen as an instructor at any stage of this school, Fétis credits him as being one of the founding teachers. From surviving payroll and personnel documents it is known that in 1795 the *Conservatoire* employed nineteen professors of clarinet and thirty performers of clarinet to teach six hundred students. The number of students rose to eight hundred and eighteen in 1798, and by 1800 the *Conservatoire de Paris* employed fifty-four clarinet teachers. Sweeping changes to the *Conservatoire* in 1802 cut both the number of teachers and students, resulting in two clarinet teachers and four hundred students. Although it is unclear what exactly Vanderhagen taught at the Conservatory, one source lists him as a French clarinet virtuoso associated with the Paris Conservatory.[50] After the drastic changes in 1802, Vanderhagen was apparently no longer associated with the *Conservatoire*.

The *Garde Nationale*, although it retained most of its original personnel, including Vanderhagen, began to undergo a series of reorganizations and name changes starting with the *Garde du Directoire* in 1795. Napoleon, upon a review of the effectiveness of the *Garde du Directoire*, issued a decree on November 28, 1799 that it would now be know as the *Garde Consulaire*. Comprised of a company of light infantry, two battalions of foot soldiers, one company of cavalry, two squadrons of light cavalry, and one company of light artillery, the

---

[48] David Whitwell, *Band Music of the French Revolution* (Tutzing, Germany: Verlegt Bei Hans Schneider, 1979), 59.

[49] Ibid., 89–90.

[50] Oskar Kroll, *The Clarinet*, trans. Hilda Morris, ed. Anthony Baines (New York: Taplinger Publishing Company, 1968), 69.

Garde Consulaire required a record of prior bravery under fire and good conduct for admission. By January 3, 1800, the *Garde Consulaire* contained over two thousand and eighty-nine men, including fifty musicians. Of these musicians twenty-five were assigned to the light infantry and the other half to the cavalry.[51]

On July 29, 1804, Napoleon created from the *Garde Consulaire* the *Garde Imperiale*, citing a need for a personal protective army. The *Garde Imperiale* was comprised of the best members of the *Garde Consulaire*, and included both a full military band and a drum and fife ensemble. Primarily stationed in Paris, the musicians of the *Garde Imperiale* were contracted employees who were eligible to leave once their terms had expired. Although only the members of the drum and fife band (part of the cavalry units) were considered to be soldiers, Napoleon treated and paid all the musicians well. Such relatively high status can be found in an examination of military rank, as the bandmaster (chief musician) and drum major (tambour-major) were both considered part of the *État-Major*, or military officers and staff whose rank was above that of colonel.[52]

In 1804 the band of the *Garde Imperiale* was comprised of twelve C clarinets and two piccolo clarinets in F.[53] This number was considerably larger than the eight total musicians permitted by regulations, but numerous records from the era of the *Garde Imperiale* indicate band sizes of two to three dozen musicians. One possible explanation for such a large ensemble comes from Napoleon's use of the band to communicate information during battle. In the face of such great noise larger ensembles would have an obvious auditory advantage.

The musicians of the *Garde Imperiale* were, with the exception of the drums and fifes, typically assigned to the first regiment of the infantry. Vanderhagen, who served as an assistant bandmaster for the *Grenadiers-à-Pied de la Garde Imperiale*, was honored for his contributions during the Prussian

---

[51] Alain Pigeard, *Dictionnaire de la Grande Armée* (Paris: Tallandier, 2002), 338.

[52] Ibid.

[53] Ibid., 422.

campaign of 1806–07, and Napoleon presented him with the *Légion d'Honneur* in 1807.[54] First created by Napoleon in 1802, this award was accompanied by a hefty monetary bonus, and recipients were required to wear their medals as part of their uniform at all times. An 1849 publication on the history of the *Gardes Nationales de France* lists an individual named Vanderhagen as a "*Mentions Honorables*" for his military service in the infantry of the 7th Legion, 4th battalion.[55]

Changes to the *Garde Imperiale* in 1808 and again in 1813 resulted in a significant reduction of personnel including the elimination of positions within the band. A listing of musicians in Paris from 1810 gives Vanderhagen's current occupation as music director for the King's Guard; this listing also credits Vanderhagen as a recipient of the *Légion d'Honneur* and the former assistant music director of the *Garde Imperiale*.[56] The defeat of Napoleon at Waterloo in June 1815 resulted in the subsequent collapse of the Empire and the dissolution of the *Garde Imperiale*.

With the loss of his military career, Vanderhagen quickly turned to other ensembles, becoming principal clarinet at the *Théâtre Français* of Paris with Gabriel Péchignier as second clarinet.[57] Vanderhagen played at the *Théâtre* from 1815–18, and in 1818 accepted an additional position at the Paris *Opéra* as second

---

[54] Pamela Weston, *More Clarinet Virtuosi of the Past* (London: Halston and Co., 1977), 262.

[55] It is unclear whether this listing refers to Amand Vanderhagen because it does not provide any identifying information beyond a surname. Although the spelling of Vanderhagen in this publication is accurate for our subject, this listing designates his status as that of captain. Amand Vanderhagen, as an assistant bandmaster, held a ranking two listings higher than captain. (MM Alboize and Charles Élic, *Fastes des Gardes Nationales de France* (Place: Chez MM. Goubaud and Laurent Olivier, 1849), 594).

[56] "VANDERHAGEN (Amand-Jean-Francois-Joseph), member de la legion d'honneur, ci-devant chef de la garde du roi, ex-sous-chef de la musique de la garde impériale et royale" (Alexandre Choron, *Dictionnaire historique des musiciens, artistes et amateurs, morts ou vivans, qui se sont illustrés et une partie quelconque de la musique et des arts qui y sont relatifs...* (Paris: Chimot, 1810), 398–99).

[57] Péchignier (1782–1853) had been one of the Paris Conservatory's first clarinet students, studying with Jean Xavier Lefèvre from 1797–1802. (Weston, 192).

clarinet.[58] Struggling with increasingly severe health problems, he switched to second clarinet at the *Théâtre* in 1818, with Hugray becoming principal.[59] Vanderhagen continued to play second clarinet in both ensembles until his death in July of 1822, with his address in 1821–22 being no. 23 *rue du Dragon*.[60] This final residence reflects Vanderhagen's wealth and status at the end of his life, as the *rue du Dragon* remains to this day one of Paris's major thoroughfares. Although his home still stands it has undergone major renovations since 1822, and today houses a boutique on the ground floor and apartments on the upper floors.

Vanderhagen's Oeuvre

Although only a few of his compositions are in print today, Vanderhagen's compositions were highly regarded during his lifetime. Choron, in his *Dictionnaire historique des musiciens, artistes et amateurs, morts ou vivans* (1810), describes Vanderhagen's music thus:

> It is this writer who has composed a great quantity of works, many for the clarinet and for the flute, including concerti, quartets, trio, and duets, all universally esteemed, especially for the beauty of their melody, their ease of execution, and their comfortable technique.[61]

This praise was later repeated or rephrased by other writers, such as John Sainsbury:

---

[58] Weston, 192.

[59] Hugray, also known as Hugrais, held the principal clarinet position with the *Théâtre* until 1830. (Weston, 134).

[60] Weston, 262.

[61] "Cet auteur a composé une grande quantité d'ouvrages, tant pour la clarinette que pour la flûte, comme concertos, quatuors, trios et duos, tous généralement estimés, tant pour la beauté duchant que pour la facilité de l'exécution et l'aissance du doigté." (Choron, 398).

He composed a vast variety of music for wind instruments, especially for the clarinet and flute. Many of his works were greatly admired, both for the beauty of their melody and harmony, and for the facility of performance.[62]

Fétis lists Vanderhagen's compositions for the military bands in which he performed and conducted:

> Skillful, in his day, in arranging music of all kinds for military band, he published several collections, among which may be noted the following: 1. Wind suites for military band in 10 parts, op.14, 17, 20, and 21; Paris, Frère. 2. Two suites of *pas redoublés* idem; Paris, Leduc. 3. Pot-pourri in 8 parts; Paris, Janet. 4. Grand military symphony; ibid. 5. Another item (for the birth of the king of Rome); ibid. 6. Three suites of airs from Italian operas for two clarinets, two horns and two bassoons; ibid.[63]

Vanderhagen's arrangements of wind suites and opera melodies given by Fétis correspond with the listing of his compositions in *Tablettes des Renommée* (1785). The collections of operatic melodies for clarinet also includes Vanderhagen's *Receuils d'ariettes choisies*, books 1 and 2, for two clarinets (c. 1783).[64] Fétis also lists additional compositions for clarinet by Vanderhagen including concertos, duos, and solos:

> 11. Concertos for the clarinet, numbers 1, 2, 3, ibid. (Paris, Sieber, Pleyel, P. Petit). 12. Seventeen sets of duos for two clarinets, Paris, at all

---

[62]John S. Sainsbury, *A Dictionary of Musicians from the Earliest Times*, vol. 2 (London: Sainsbury and Co., 1825; reprint, New York: Da Capo Press, 1966), 500. Sainsbury refers to all clarinetists as performers on the *clarionet*: "Lefevre, Xavier, an excellent performer on the clarionet" (ibid., 55).

[63] "Habile, pour son temps, dans l'arrangement de toute espèce de musique en harmonie militarie, il en a publie plusieurs recueils parmi lesquels on remarque: 1. Suites d'harmonic militaire à 10 parties, op.14, 17, 20 et 21, Paris, Frère. 2. Deux suites de pas redoublés *idem*, Paris, Leduc. 3. Pot-pourri à 8 parties, Paris, Janet. 4. Grande symphonie militaire, *ibid*. 5. Autre *idem* (la naissance du roi de Rome), *ibid*. 6. Trois suites d'airs d'opéras Italiens pour 2 clarinettes, 2 cors et 2 bassons, *ibid*" (Fétis, 431).

[64] Weston, 262.

publishers. 13. Many varied and assorted melodies for the same instrument, ibid.[65]

Choron also credits Vanderhagen for writing and arranging numerous works for military band, including opera overtures and arias, as well as selections from Haydn's *Creation*. Other listed compositions include forty fanfares for four trumpets and tympani and *La naissance du roi de Rome*, a military symphony for large orchestra dedicated to the army. This latter work, scored for C and F clarinets, flute, horn, trumpet, bassoon, serpent, trombone, bass drum, and cymbals, was composed between 1811–12 to celebrate the birth of Napoleon's son on March 20, 1811.

Other works listed by Choron as belonging to Vanderhagen's *oeuvre* include:

1) A great military symphony concertante for clarinet, flute, horn, bassoon, and violin obligato; 2) a great military symphony for twelve wind instruments; 3) six trios for two flutes and alto; 4) lots of military marches in double time, and waltzes for all of the instruments employed in the regiment bands.[66]

Sainsbury mentions that Vanderhagen also "composed some vocal music."[67] One of these works, *An Invocation to Friendship*, for large choir and orchestra, was likely written for one of the numerous patriotic celebrations given between 1792 and 1800. Other vocal works include the *Romance of Estelle* and the *Romance of Gonzalve of Cordoue*, which were based upon the pastoral

---

[65] "11. Concertos pour la clarinette, nos 1, 2, 3, *ibid*. (Paris, Sieber, Pleyel, P. Petit). 12. Dix-sept œuvres de duos pour 2 clarinettes, a Paris, chez tous les éditeurs. 13. Beaucoup d'airs variés et de pots-pourris pour le même instrument, *ibid*" (Fétis, 431).

[66] "1°. Une grande symphonie concertante pour clarinette, flûte, cor, bassoon, et violon oblige; 2°. Une grande symphonie militaire pour douze instrumens à vent; 3°. Six trios pour deux flûtes et alto; 4°. Beaucoup de marches militaries, pas redoubles, et Valzes avec tous les instrumens qu'on emploie dans les regimens." (Choron., 399).

[67] Sainsbury, 500.

23

romances of Jean-Pierre Claris de Florian (1755–1794), a popular French poet and romance writer who published *Estelle* in 1788 and *Gonzalve de Cordoue* in 1791. He died as a result of incarceration during the Revolution. Because neither of these two compositions survive, it is not known if Vanderhagen wrote these works as operas or oratorios.

A third known work, *Lettres à Emilie sur la Mythologie*, is based upon a work of the same title by Charles-Albert Demoustier (1760–1801) who wrote it in six parts, beginning in 1786 and finishing in 1798. His decision to cast the work in alternating prose and madrigal-like verses made it extremely popular and became the basis for a new style of writing in France.

Vanderhagen dedicated several of his early instrumental works to various important members of the nobility who were closely associated with the royal court. His *Six Duos concertans pour deux flûtes*, 1780, is dedicated to "M. le Comte d'Esterhasy, brigadier des Armées du Roi, Mestre de camp."[68] A relative of the Esterhazy family of Austria, the Comte was an extremely close friend of the Queen and was present for the birth of her first child. Vanderhagen dedicated a second set of flute duos, *6 Duos concertans pour 2 flûtes*, to another dear friend of the Queen's, Madame de Kerdavy, in 1784.[69] It would seem that these flute duets were very popular at the royal court, as Vanderhagen dedicated a third set of

---

[68] Six Duos concertans pour deux flûtes; dédiés à M. le Comte d'Esterhasy, brigadier des Armées du Roi, Mestre de camp, par A. VANDERHAGEN, œuvre 2ème, Prix 7 liv. 4 s. [Ces duos ne sont pas d'une grande difficulté quoique l'auteur y ait placé quelquefois des traits fort propres à arrêter les commençans & à les exercer par là, d'une manière profitable (*Announces, affiches et avis divers*)]. A Paris, chez Baillon, successeur de M. Jolivet, M^d de musique de la Reine, rue Françoise près de la Comédie italienne, à la Muse lyrique (*Journal de Paris* 5 April 1780; *Gazette de France* 11 April 1780 (p. 142); *Journal de la Librairie* 22 April 1780; *Announces, affiches et avis divers* 27 April 1780 (p. 974)).

[69] 6 Duos concertans pour 2 flûtes par Amand VANDERHAGEN, musicien au Régiment des Gardes-Françoises, dédiés à Mme de Kerdavy. Œuvre IV. Prix 7 liv. 4 s. Chez Baillon, rue neuve des Petits-champs (*Journal de Paris* 28 November 1783; *Journal de la Librairie* 6 December 1783; *Announces, affiches et avis divers* 9 December 1783 (p. 2939); *Mercure de France* 17 January 1784 (p. 144)).

6 duos concertans pour 2 flûtes to M. le comte de Vergennes,[70] a foreign ambassador for France and a highly regarded public official. Vanderhagen's dedication to the Comte, also known as Gravier, is one given in memoriam, as Gravier died suddenly on February 13, 1787 (these duets were first mentioned in a print advertisement in July 1787).[71] An earlier dedication to the Comte de Vergennes, *2de Suite d'airs connus en quatuor pour clarinette, basson ou violoncelle, violon et alto* (April-May 1784), was likely inspired by Gravier's return that spring from his visit to the fledgling United States.[72]

Although there is no question that Vanderhagen wrote numerous works for the military bands in which he played and conducted, few records of these compositions remain. Many of Vanderhagen's works for military band have been lost due to the widespread destruction of archival documents during the French Revolution and the Paris Commune of 1871. Based on their instrumentation, it can be assumed that works such as the *Suite d'airs d'harmonie, arranges pour 2 clarinettes, 2 cors et 2 bassons* (1786), 1ème Suite d'*Amusemens militaries en harmonie pour 2 cors, 2 clarinettes & 2 bassons, contenant les airs de la Colonie & autres* (1776), and *Ouverture d'Iphigénie en Aulide et Carillon des Trois Fermiers en harmonie pour deux clarinettes, deux cors et deux bassoons* (1781) were scored for military bands or their smaller ensembles. Vanderhagen also wrote and edited the *Journal d'harmonie militaire*, which contained various marches and arrangements of popular opera melodies for the small military band combination of two clarinets, two horns, and bassoons. Vanderhagen produced

---

[70] 6 duos concertans pour 2 flûtes; dédiés à M. le comte de Vergennes, ...par Amand VADER-HAGEN [sic], musicien de la garde française de S.M. Œuvre 12ème et 5ème livre de duo de flute. Prix 7 liv. 4 s. port franc. Chez Baillon, rue du Petit Reposoir, près de la Place des Victoires (*Journal de la Librairie* 16 June 1787; *Journal de Paris* 25 June 1787; *Gazette de France* 24 July 1787; *Announces, affiches et avis divers* 29 July 1787 (p. 2126)).

[71] Ibid.

[72] 2de Suite d'airs connus en quatuor pour clarinette, bassoon ou violoncelle, violon et alto par M. VAN DER HAGEN, dédiés au chevalier de Vergennes. A Paris, chez Boyer, rue Neuve des Petits-Champs et chez Mme Le Menu, rue du Roule (*Journal de Paris* 29 April 1784; *Journal de la Librairie* 22 May 1784)).

this journal from 1777 until 1800, with each issue being described as "for use by the regimens [bands]."[73] The size of this particular publication was reflected in its price of sixty livres; Vanderhagen's other works during this time, such as his flute and clarinet duets, rarely sold for more than seven livres. While the majority of Vanderhagen's music published before 1800 credits him as being a "musicien du Roi," none of his work published after 1800 acknowledges his involvement in any military band. This may be the result of personal or general public sentiments during and after the French Revolution towards royalty and *l'Ancien Régime*.

Vanderhagen's clarinet treatises and pedagogy are not mentioned with any particular detail in any of his biographical sources. For example, Fétis mentions only two of Vanderhagen's Methods:

> Nouvelle méthode de clarinette, contenant les premiers eléménts de la musique et les principes pour bien jouer de cet instrument; Paris, Pleyel. Nouvelle méthode pour la clarinette moderne à douze clefs, avec leur application aux notes essentielles, etc., Paris, Pleyel and Naderman.[74]

Choron goes a step further to credit Vanderhagen as the first to create elementary works for the clarinet and flute:

> He is also the first to create elementary works for the instruments cited above, which are: two sensible methods for the clarinet, two of the same for the flute, and one for the oboe. These methods are extremely clear and easy, filled with a great quantity of lessons, which gradually teach the student, from the gamut to great difficulties.[75]

---

[73] *Journal d'harmonie militaire*, contenant un choix d'ariettes extraites des opera-comiques, accomodées pour 2 clarinettes, 2 cors de chasse & 2 bassons par Amand VANDERAGEN, musicien des Gardes-françoises, à l'usage des regimens. Prix 60 liv. Il paroîtra douze recueils... dans le courant. On est en état de délivrer les cinq premiers mois d'avance. Chez le sieur de La Chevardière, rue du Roule (*Announces, affiches et avis divers* 9 January 1777 (p. 41)).

[74] "16. *Nouvelle méthode de clarinette, contenant les premiers eléménts de la musique et les principes pour bien jouer de cet instrument*, Paris, Pleyel. 17. *Nouvelle méthode pour la clarinette moderne à douze clefs, avec leur application aux notes essentielles*, etc., Paris, Pleyel et Naderman" (Fétis, 431).

[75] "Il est aussie le premier qui ait fait des ouvrages élémentaires pour les instrumens cités ci-dessus, savoir: deux methods raisonnées pour la clarinette, deux *idem* pour la flûte et une pour

Nouvelle méthode de clarinette is assumed to be Vanderhagen's second treatise from 1799, while Pleyel published *Nouvelle méthode pour la clarinette moderne à douze clefs* posthumously in 1827. *Nouvelle méthode pour la clarinette moderne à douze clefs* was published earlier in 1819 by Pleyel & Fils aîné, and cited in the *Journal general de la literature de France*, Année 22 (1819).[76] It is possible that, given the popularity of other clarinet methods by authors like Lefèvre at this time, Vanderhagen's third method failed to sell and was taken out of circulation, being sold to Pleyel sometime between 1819 and 1827. Pleyel may have offered it posthumously in an attempt to capitalize on Vanderhagen's recent death and former reputation.

Vanderhagen's first clarinet treatise, *Méthode nouvelle et raisonnée pour la clarinette* (1785), was so popular that it appeared in several competing editions.[77] Nadermann (ca. 1797–98), and Sieber (ca. 1799 and ca. 1802–03) both published later editions of this work. The existence of multiple editions also applies to the second treatise, *Nouvelle méthode pour la clarinette*, with three different editions that were published around 1800 by Pleyel, and Naderman. *Nouvelle méthode pour la clarinette* was reprinted several more times during the first half of the nineteenth century, with later editions by Renato Meucci (1800, Italian translation), Pleyel & Fils aîné (1816, marked "2eme Edition"), Pleyel (1828, English translation), and Breitkopf & Härtel (1834, French and German texts). The earliest publication date known for this treatise is 1799 by Pleyel, which is the edition used for this research. It is likely that Agostino Gabucci was referring to one of these pirated copies when he mentions "F. Vanderhagen

---

le hautbois. Ces methods sont extrémement claires et faciles, remplies d'une grande quantité de leçons qui conduisent graduellement l'éléve, depuis la gamme jus-qu'au grandes difficultés." (Choron, 398).

[76] "Nouvelle méthode pour la clarinette moderne a 12 clef...suivie de tous les principes de musiques...lecons graduees...avec des airs...des duos, des polonaises, des airs variés & plusieurs études. Gravée par C. Marie. 19 February 1819." (*Journal general de la literature de France*, Annee 22 (1819)).

[77] Weston, 262.

(1793–1832), a German, renowned for his Methods."[78] The popularity and impact of these clarinet treatises even led to the creation of a method book that acknowledged its reliance on Vanderhagen's work, Philippe Berr's *Nouvelle Méthode de Clarinette à 6 et à 13 cles, d'après celle de Vanderhagen*.[79] Berr includes fingering charts for both a six and thirteen-keyed clarinet.

Little credit has been given to Vanderhagen for his flute and oboe methods, either by his contemporaries or modern authors. Sainsbury is the only early source that mentions Vanderhagen's non-clarinet treatises, including one for oboe:

> His *Méthode nouvelle et raisonnée pour le Hautbois diviée en 2 Parties, Paris, 1798*, is considered to be one of the very best instruction books for that instrument. His introductions to the flute and to the clarionet are also highly spoken of: the title of the former is *Méthode Claire et facile pour apprendre à jouer en très-peu de temps de la Flûte*, Paris, 1798.[80]

Fétis mentions Vanderhagen's music for flute, as well as other winds, in the supplement to his *Biographie Universelle*:

> He published a collection of twelve short airs and six duos for two flutes, another collection of duos for six flutes taken from comic operas; also the melodies from *Une Folie*, by Mehul, arranged for wind band, and songs from *Picaros et Diego*, by Dalayrac, also arranged for winds.[81]

---

[78] Gabucci's "F." may stand for Vanderhagen's middle name, François, although all other references to Vanderhagen use his given name, Amand. He also gives Vanderhagen's dates as 1793–1832. (Agostino Gabucci, *Origin and History of the Clarinet*, 3rd rev. ed., trans. Frederic Lubrani (Memphis: Memphis State University, 1969), 46).

[79] Berr, Philippe, *Nouvelle Méthode de Clarinette à 6 et à 13 cles, d'après celle de Vanderhagen* (Paris: Aulagnier, 1832–44).

[80] Sainsbury, 500.

[81] "Il publia un recueil de *Douze petits airs et six duos pour 2 flûtes*, un autre recueil de Duos pour 6 flûtes tirés des opéras-comiques, puis les airs d *Une Folie*, de Mehul, mis en harmonie, et les airs de *Picaros et Diego*, de Dalayrac, mis en harmonie" (Fétis, *Biographie Universelle des Musiciens et Bibliographie Générale de la Musique, Supplément et Complément*, vol. 2 (Paris: Librairie de Firmin-Didot, 1881), 601).

Despite Vanderhagen's numerous compositions,[82] only a few works are extant today, including some duets for clarinet and flute, as well as his treatises for clarinet, flute, and oboe.[83]

---

[82] Please refer to Appendix One for a list of all known compositions by Vanderhagen.

[83] Please refer to Appendix Two for a list representing Vanderhagen's oeuvre and publications that contain music by Vanderhagen currently available in print. At this time no discography for Vanderhagen exists.

Chapter 2

Méthode nouvelle et raisonnée pour la clarinette (1785)

In order to demonstrate Vanderhagen's importance as a clarinet pedagogue, the following two chapters provide complete translations of his first two instructional treatises on the clarinet, *Méthode nouvelle et raisonnée pour la clarinette* (1785) and *Nouvelle méthode de clarinette* (1799). These translations have been prepared from copies of the original manuscripts kept at the Bibliothèque nationale de France (BnF). I have attempted in these translations to preserve as much of Vanderhagen's writing style as possible. Inconsistencies in punctuation and the presence of extended run-on sentences in some sections has required me to break passages into smaller sentences in order to make the material understandable. A discrepancy occurs in Vanderhagen's use of numbers because they are presented both as numerals and are spelled out; these appear in my translation as they are found in the treatises. Footnotes are given at certain points to explain translational difficulties including archaic terms, misspellings, and ambiguous phrases. My goal has been to create translations that are easily understandable in modern English, yet retain their eighteenth-century French character.

Méthode nouvelle et raisonnée pour la clarinette (1785)

MÉTHODE
Nouvelle et Raisonnée
POUR LA CLARINETTE

Ou l'on donne une explication claire et succinte de la maniere de tenir cet Instrument, de son étendue, de son embouchure, de la qualité des anches que les Commençans doivent employer, du vrai son, des coups de langue, et en général de tout ce qui a raport à la Clarinette. Cette Méthode renferme aussi quelques leçons ou les différens coups de langue sont mis en pratique, douze petits Airs et six Duo très propres à former les Eleves.

AMAND VAN-DER-HAGEN
Musicien de la Garde françoise Ordinaire du Roy.

Prix 9.l

A PARIS

Chez M.' Boyer, Rue de Richelieu, à la Clef d'Or,
à l'ancien Caffé de foy.
Chez Mad.' Le Menu, Rue du Roule, à la Clef d'Or.

Reprinted, by permission of the BnF, from Vanderhagen, *Methode nouvelle et raisonnee pour la clarinette* (1785), title page.

New and Explained Method for the Clarinet

Where is given a clear and succinct explanation on how to hold this instrument, of its range, of its embouchure, of the quality of reeds which beginners should use, of its true sound, of tonguing, and in general of all that concerns the clarinet.[84] This method also contains some lessons where the different articulations are put into practice, with twelve small airs and six duos very appropriate for training students.

Amand Vanderhagen, Musician in the French Ordinary Guard of the King

Price: 9 Livres

Paris

Published by Monsieur Boyer, *Rue de Richelieu*, at *Clef d'Or*, in the ancient *Caffé de foy*

and by Mademoiselle Le Menu, *Rue du Roule*, at the *Clef d'Or*

---

[84] I have translated *Coups de langue* as "tonguing"; its literal translation is "strokes of the tongue."

32

The Natural Scale

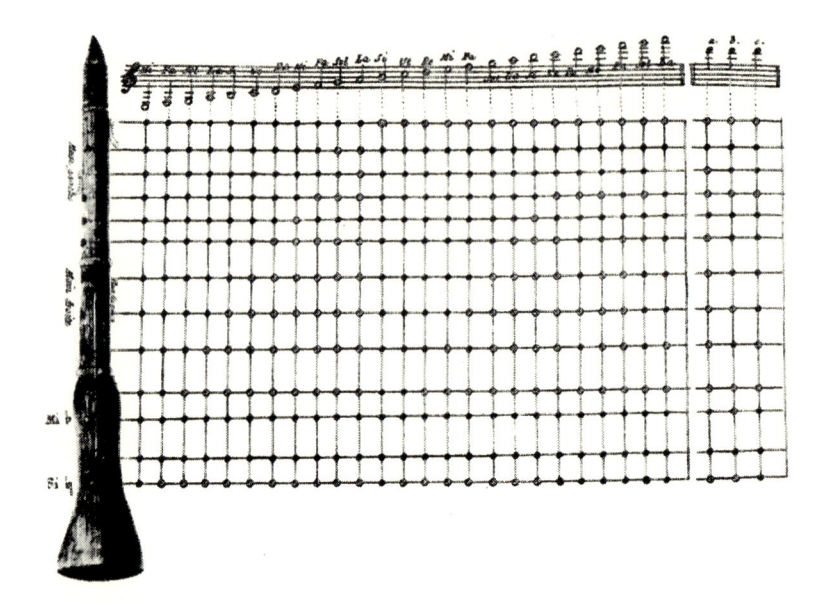

Reprinted, by permission of the BnF, from Vanderhagen, *Methode nouvelle et raisonnee pour la clarinette* (1785), 2.

The black dots indicate closed holes and the whites open holes. The top note, F, is only slightly useful. There are three different positions for producing D. The diagram of the clarinet illustrates the left-hand and right-hand joints on the front of the instrument and the thumbhole on the back.

33

Scale of Sharps and Flats

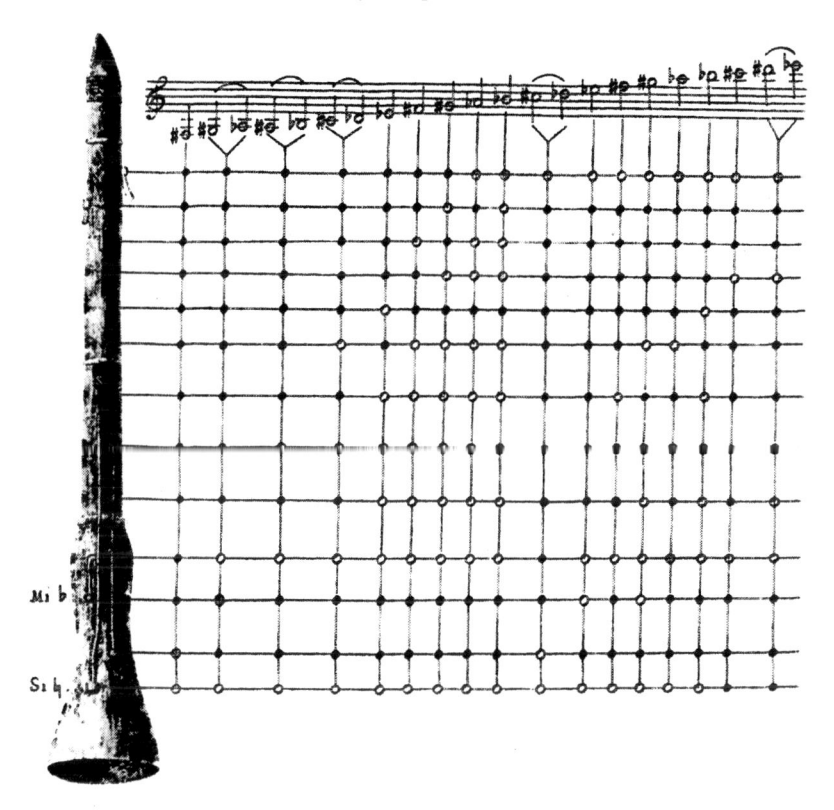

Reprinted, by permission of the BnF, from Vanderhagen, *Methode nouvelle et raisonnee pour la clarinette* (1785), 3.

The chromatic notes are always indeterminate. Moreover, of all of the instruments I speak of the clarinet, as they do not descend by the same positions. It is the ear of the student that gives guidance, because nothing is more difficult on the clarinet than the semitones, especially those in the high register.

First Article (and the most essential): The Position of the Arms and the Head

This article is very interesting for beginners, as much for acquiring grace in playing as for avoiding the problems that ordinarily result from poor posture. We must then, in carrying the clarinet to the mouth, neither raise nor lower our heads because this impedes breathing freely. We must hold our heads naturally straight without affectation, with the left elbow 5 or 6 inches from the body and the right elbow a little more elevated, so that the bottom of the clarinet is nearly a foot and a half from the body, with the fingers extended on the holes and the two wrists a bit flexible. The holes can now be stopped more easily, for in elevating the wrists and the elbows space is created under the finger and the thumb of the right hand beneath the clarinet, between the first and the second finger. The thumb of the left hand must always be ready to take up the key, or to stop the hole, and consequently must make only very small movements. It is the same for the fingers in general, as we should lift the fingers only a very small distance from the instrument, and always perpendicularly, so that the two hands are always able to lean towards the wood of the clarinet.[85] None of the fingers should touch each other so they can cadence freely. It is also necessary when a finger or several fingers are lifted, that they remain perpendicular above the holes that they must close, for in withdrawing them like many students do, they always have trouble relocating the holes and that impedes execution.

Second Article: On the Embouchure

The embouchure is the basis of all the wind instruments. My object being to discuss that of the clarinet, I will then say that we must not have too much embouchure on the mouthpiece of the clarinet, but only up to the shoulder of the reed.[86] By extending the clarinet [mouthpiece] too far into the mouth we lose the means of controlling it because it causes pinching which occurs because of a lack of elasticity. The reed is applied on the mouthpiece towards the ligature, and can thus no longer act. We must not then engage the instrument except as I have said previously, by supporting the mouthpiece on the teeth, and covering the reed with the upper lip without the teeth of the upper jaw touching in any circumstance.

---

[85] Engraver mistake: *pancher* should be *pencher*, "to lean."

[86] I have translated *défaut de la taille de l'anche* as "up to the shoulder of the reed"; its literal translation is "up to the cut in the reed."

35

Because the teeth support and give strength to the upper lip for holding in the high notes, it is also necessary that the sides of the mouth be very firm in order not to allow wind to exit the sides of the embouchure. In beginning the scale for the lowest range of the clarinet, we should not pinch by any means, but only hold the reed with the lips in order to prevent squeaks, and upon arriving at the second octave, which will begin on E, , begin to pinch gradually. We will observe the same movement in descending, that is to say, in loosening the lips bit by bit, but always by controlling the reed in order to avoid certain disagreeable squeaks which are rather frequent on this instrument when we pinch too much in the middle and too little in the high notes.

Third Article: The Quality of Reeds for Beginners

A beginner must not use a strong reed because it makes the instrument more resistant for him than is effective and because his lips are not yet accustomed to pinching. Strong reeds can also make the clarinet screech and cause it to lose a lot of air through both sides of the mouth. It is necessary then to make a soft reed for the beginner, but not too weak because the sound will resemble a duck. We must test the chalumeau of the clarinet[87] by moving from E, , up to E, .[88] If all of these notes come out well and velvety and without squawking, the others will come out the same, at least up to high C [C^6] or D [D^6]. Although an ambitious student may want to ascend to F [F^6], G [G^6], or A [A^6], only when he has acquired firmness in the lips will he succeed. Moreover these three extreme notes are not beautiful on the instrument

---

[87] The chalumeau here refers to the first octave range of the clarinet.

[88] Vanderhagen notates the two notes by showing them below and on the staff (E^2 and E^3, respectively, where C^3 represents middle C on the piano).

and are practiced rarely except in concertos or in bits of etudes where they are still very controlled.

Fourth Article: Manner of Acquiring a Good Sound

The beauty of the clarinet is in the production of a good sound. This is essential, and we can give pleasure with this instrument even in mediocre playing. Not all connoisseurs will approve this last sentence because they have often had proof of the contrary, but this proof proceeds only from a poor choice of music played by beginners, for scarcely have beginners left their teachers when they play particular bits of music absolutely out of their reach. If they choose melodic, less difficult pieces, they then prove that a good well-sustained sound will take the place of the great difficulties that they cannot execute and that make their listeners suffer. Let us return to this subject in my fourth chapter.

For acquiring a beautiful sound, do not try to roll your fingers on the instrument, but on the contrary, play the scale very slowly and swell the sound of each note. When you play the scale, play also *Adagio* or *Andante*, and finally all melodic pieces, banishing *Allegro* and *Presto* until you are sure of the sound and of the fingers. I know through experience that all students try to roll their fingers on the entire length of the instrument. This is a great abuse, for besides not knowing what they are doing, articulations, the fingers, and finally everything else becomes a contradiction. Here is an example of a scale that I want you to look over. Sustain each note as much as your lungs will permit and begin each note with very little air and then swell gradually.

Beginners learning the scale, or even some short lessons, must take care never to play with partial air support for they will draw out the loudest possible sound. Once they have produced a loud sound, they should then attempt to sweeten it by the means indicated above.[89]

Fifth Article: Different Articulations

Articulation is to wind instruments what the bow stroke is to string instruments. It is the different strokes of the tongue[90] that produce articulation. We will begin with the ordinary articulation that must be pronounced "D" to forming a connection between all the notes.

- Example: When there is nothing marked on the note, we express them on "D."

- Expressing on "T": When we find dots above the notes this is comparable to an articulated or detached bowed stroke.

- Another example A: This articulation is very beautiful when we do it well. It is necessary to slur the first two notes and give two strokes of the tongue on the two final ones and so on to slightly mark the first of the fours. This is a common articulation.

---

[89] I have translated *à demi jeu* as "to play with partial [air] support"; its literal translation is "to half play." Vanderhagen in his *Nouvelle methode de clarinette* (1799) defines *mezzoforte* as *à demi jeu*.

[90] I have translated *coups de langue* as "strokes of the tongue."

- Another example[91]: When the passage begins with three notes, it is necessary to use three tongue strokes for the rest.

- Another example: The first tongued and the three others slurred.[92]

- Another example: The first three slurred and the last tongued.

- Another example: Melodic types. Notes slurred two-by-two.

Example for Very Rapid Passages

When the movement of a piece is too fast, we do not use the tonguing pattern of two slurred [notes] with two tongued [notes], but we can use the above example successfully by always emphasizing the first note and by expressing the others from the depth of the lungs, but only in difficult situations. In other cases we should practice Example A even in melodic phrases.

---

[91] I have translated *autre* as "another example"; its literal translation is "another."

[92] I have translated *piqué* as "tongued"; its literal translation is "spiked."

Observation

There are other tongue strokes, but as they can be derived only from the ones I have mentioned, teachers will teach them to students as the circumstances present themselves. I do not claim to speak of what the others may require, and I want to alert the student to the signs that announce this or that articulation so that they may play them as they have found them marked. For example, if we find neither slurs nor tonguing in a passage, it is necessary to begin by slurring the first two and connecting articulations, that is to say, expressed by D on all of them if the measure is found to be in triple meter.

- Example

Sixth Article: Triplets or Three-in-One

There are also different ways of making triplets by using the articulations of which I am going to give an example. Let us never forget to give a little more expression to the first note of three, and it is a general rule that in such a manner the notes are linked together, either by two-by-three or by four-by-six. The first should be marked more than the others.

- Example: articulation linked by "D."

- Another example: articulation detached by "T."

The difference in these strokes is perceptible. These expressions by "D" do not leave silence, and they prolong the sound from one note to another. The tongue strokes that are detached and pronounced by "T" seem to leave a small rest between each note because of the dry attack that the letter "T" produces.

- Another example: The first two are slurred and the last tongued. This articulation is often practical, and we must learn it.

- Another example: It happens often that we cannot make these three notes at the same time because another instrument articulates them first, for then there remains only the two slurred final notes seen in the following example.

- Example: The expression of the first note after the half breath must be barely perceptible, and diminished on the second as indicated by the sign >, because in every slur the first should have more force than the last.

- Another example: Mixed example of three different articulations.

- Another example: All are slurred; but in order to distinguish three-by-three, it is necessary to emphasize the first, not by a small tongue stroke, but by a small expression of the throat, because in marking the first note too much by tonguing it compares to this:

- Another example: Six-in-two: we must avoid rendering this as three-for-one by not giving expression on the fourth note. The first alone must carry the expression, and it is necessary to observe the same principle in the case where linking by six is necessary.

Seventh Article: Appoggiaturas[93]

An appoggiatura is a note of embellishment that we can add or that is often found between two notes that succeed each other diatonically in ascension. The extension of a tone serves as repetition from the first note to that which succeeds it, and it must always be tied with the note that follows it.

---

[93] I have translated *port de voix* as "appoggiatura"; its literal translation is "carrying the voice" or "extended tones."

- Example: Appoggiatura; its value and expression.

- On the same subject.

Eighth Article: The Accent

The accent is therefore a note of embellishment that is found or is added sometimes at the end of a note in order to make a song more graceful. The accent is formed ordinarily by a note diatonically above, or even at the third above, the one that we want to make heard. It serves to distinguish and to reunite at the same time the expression of the note that precedes it with that note which follows. In order to determine the force that must be given to it, it is only a matter of making it heard imperceptibly as if it were the prolongation of a sustained sound.

43

- Example: It is good to observe that all of these examples have no determined tempo. We can play them more or less at will. We will give several movements of the same example.

Ninth Article: Grace Notes[94]

When a small note is found before a principal note that serves to form a melody (which we call a grace note) this small note must in all cases be slurred to the principal note. We use grace notes in different cases, but principally when we descend by thirds or when the intervals are replaced by some grace notes. Natural taste often adds this embellishment although there may be none indicated by the composer. There are, however, some cases to which nothing can be added, as in a tutti of a great orchestra where all of the instruments are ascending or descending at one time, for example , and other similar cases where we can purely and simply play the written notes. Grace notes must be practiced only in the phrases of pieces and above all when you are playing alone. Two instruments playing the same part, although able to play well separately, certainly create a bad effect when their manner of expression is

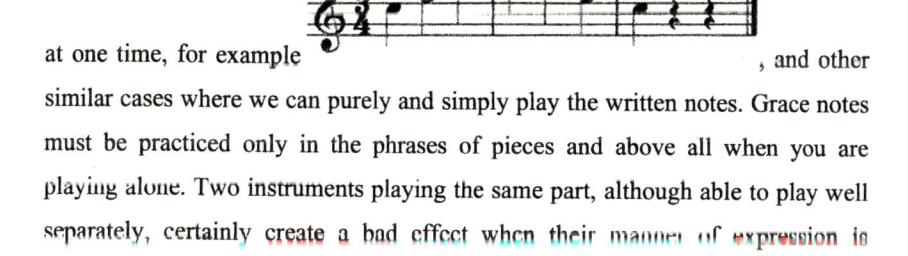

---

[94] I have translated *notes de gout* as "grace notes"; its literal translation is "notes of taste."

different. It is necessary in such cases to avoid what we call embellishment, never adding to it, and holding ourselves strictly to the note.

- Examples:

For the expression of:

- For the end of a melody we ordinarily use the expression 𝄋 by making the duration of a small note two beats through reducing the tonic note.

Tenth Article

As it is very important and even very convenient to understand reeds, I want to discuss the method of making them and how the wood for them is chosen. Reeds are of reed or cane. It is necessary to choose those that are spongy, but well dried and having veins that are neither too large nor too fine. A mouthpiece should have a width of fourteen to sixteen lines.[95] The mouthpiece should not be so large that taking hold of it constricts the reed when we press on it in order to

---

[95] Lines refers to an unspecified unit of measurement, probably comparable to the modern millimeter.

unify and equalize [the sound].[96] This operation occurs after having rough-hewn the reed and measuring it on the mouthpiece; then we position the reed by putting the two first fingers on it and sliding it onto the mouthpiece until it is well-connected below, whereupon we attach it to the mouthpiece and begin to trim its backside in order to reduce a point or degree of force so that it agrees with the embouchure.[97] It is advisable not to make a reed too weak. We should play it for one or two days, allowing its effects to appear, for then we will be able to diminish it a bit, if it is too strong. The reed must not recline too much on the mouth because this diminishes the sound too much and blocks the venting of the chalumeau or the bass of the clarinet.[98] An overly elevated reed also sounds unpleasant because it makes the instrument too shrill. We must take the middle of these two extremes and give only a half point of elevation. The sound will be very velvety.

Eleventh Article: Trills[99]

The trill is the movement of one or two fingers that must move rapidly in order to produce an equal and well-sustained attack. The trill can last only as long as the indicated value of the trill note. Borrowing a diatonic note above the note we want to trill makes the trill, and this borrowed note may be either major or minor according to the mode in which we are playing. When the trill is long we must speed up the movement of the finger toward the end and conclude quickly. I have said previously that the trill is the agitation of one or two fingers because we use two fingers (R1 and R3) for trilling on F-natural.

---

[96] Word omitted in original; reconstruction mine.

[97] Mouthpiece and reed.

[98] "Venting" refers to the channeling of air through the clarinet to produce a tone.

[99] *Cadences* has been translated as "trills;" its literal translation is "cadences."

- Trill on G, the A is the upper auxiliary note.

- Trill on F by two fingers, G is the borrowed note.

The Prepared Trill

Preparing a trill is done before articulating it by lingering for a bit of time on the upper auxiliary note.

- Example:

- Sudden or Non-Prepared [Main Note] Trill:

The difference between the sudden trill and the prepared trill consists in not preparing at all for the sudden trill, but in attacking it all at once. The trill in A, , uses all the closed holes except for the two high keys, and we can close the hole in the middle with the second finger of the right hand (R2) or the first of the left hand (L1).

47

Twelfth Article: The Mordent[100]

The mordent is the opposite of the trill on the subject of the borrowed note. It is a matter here of borrowing the note below the one that must be the mordent. The trill begins on the borrowed note, while the mordent as an opposite begins on the harmony [main] note, but like the trill the mordent finishes on the harmony note. The mordent is marked thus.

- Examples:

Before succeeding at these lessons it is advisable, in this case, to make the D (D^6) higher with the small key of A: this is because the D (D^6) is preceded or followed by C (C^6).[101] The small key is also used to make the trill on C (C^6).

- Example:

But in this case where D would be a tongued note or one sustained, it would be necessary to use one of the other positions indicated on the scale.

---

[100] I have translated *martellement* as "mordent", its literal translation is "brilliance."

[101] Vanderhagen here shows a careful consideration of pitch and offers a very useful fingering.

Scales in All Time Signatures[102]

This measure is composed of two strong beats and two weak ones; the first and third beats are stronger and the second and fourth beats are weaker.

- Measure in Four Beats: Equal Notes

These scales in different movements assist the knowledge of different measures and therefore of tonguing. This one is much easier in that all the notes are equal and ascend only by degree so that the student does not need to be occupied in the measure by always tonguing the first note of the measure.

- Measure in two beats: notes composed equally of a strong beat and a weak beat. The first note is a strong beat and the second a weak beat.

- Measure in 6/8: unequal notes:

This one is composed of two long breves, which are the quarter notes, and of two short breves, which are the eighth notes; it is necessary always to hasten the short against the long.

---

[102] I have translated *tems* as "time signature"; its literal translation is "times."

49

- Measure in three quarter notes: notes equally composed of a strong beat and two weak beats; the first note is a strong beat and the others are weak beats.

- Measure in 3/8: this measure is equal to 3/4, except that we follow it in very fast motion.

Lessons

- Measure in four beats: the whole notes are equal notes; they are worth four quarter notes.

50

It is necessary to play this scale slowly at first and go more quickly in repeating it.[103] The student should also alternate between the whole notes and quarter notes so that the essence of the principal note can be understood very easily.[104]

- Measure in two beats:

All of these lessons have no determined motion. We should play all of them *Adagio, Andante, Allegro,* and *Presto* according to the agility of the fingers, but we should always begin *Adagio.*

---

[103] Engraver mistake: *Il faut dire*, "it is necessary to say," should be *Il faut joue*, "it is necessary to play."

[104] I have translated *les valeurs* as "quarter notes"; its literal translation is "values."

- Measure in two beats:

- Measure in three beats:

- Measure in 3/8: this measure is related to that in three beats, but its motion is much faster.

- Measure in 6/8: this measure is related to that in two beats as it divides itself similarly but its motion is more playful.

- Unequal notes:

- Syncopation:

- Syncopation:

- Syncopation:

Lesson on Dotted Notes[105]

The dot can lengthen the value of half of the note that precedes it. This rule is general for all note values.

- Lesson: mixing notes of different values.

---

[105] I have translated *pointée* as "dotted notes"; its literal translation is "points."

53

- Of the same type:

- Lesson for quarter rests:

- Lesson for half quarter [eighth-note] rests:

- Half quarter rests against the beat:

- Lesson on the sixteenth rest[106]:

Examples are for transposition: this is necessary for those who want to play parts of symphonies or accompany in concerts. The clarinet in D will be used only very rarely for it is too shrill, unless it is used in those pieces that make noise. In gentle pieces, we use the clarinet in A as indicated below.

- In C: C is the natural pitch and the C clarinet plays beginning on C.

---

[106] I have translated *le quart de soupir* as "sixteenth note"; its literal translation is " a quarter of a quarter note."

55

- In D: The D clarinet plays beginning on C; this [key] is good for quick pieces.

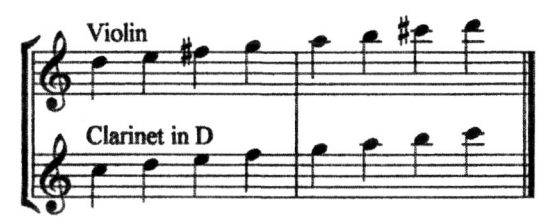

- In D: For a sweet tone the A clarinet plays beginning on F.

- In E♭: The clarinet in B♭ begins on F.

- In C minor: The clarinet in B♭ begins on D.

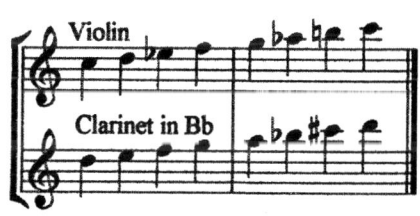

- In E♯: The clarinet in B begins on F.

- In A: The clarinet in A begins to play on C.

- In B: The clarinet in B♭ begins on C.

- In G minor: The clarinet in B♭ begins on A.

- In B♯ minor: The clarinet in B begins to play on C.

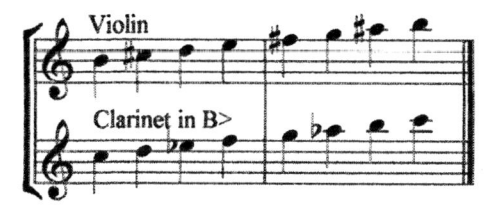

I have indicated only the tones that require transposition except the tone of C. For the others, like the tone of F and A minor, are played with the C clarinet, as well as the tone of G major and the same in minor since in most cases these are oboe parts. Since flute parts ascend too high it always necessary to transpose higher by one or two tones. We do not want to be embarrassed when we have to play with the flute for we can play the parts of the flute with the clarinet and those of the oboe with the clarinet.[107]

---

[107] Engraver mistake: *les parties de flûte avec la flûte* should be *les parties de flûte avec la clarinette*.

Twelve Small Airs for the Clarinet

Renaud's *March of the Circassienes*

The Plague of Riches (*The fresh and red rose*)

The Romance of Blaise and Babet (*It is for you that I have arranged this*)

The Two [Twin] Brothers (*The trust that you have promised me*)

Andantino (*Deign to listen*)

The Loves of Summer (*Where the day is more distant*)

Blaise and Babet (*Reading songs in the meadow*)

The Corsair (*Who is distant from you*)

Blaise and Babet (*Singing a hymn*)

Malbrouk

The Loves of Summer (*Resting for a moment*)

Legerement (*It is therefore tomorrow*)

Six Duets

Duet 1

71

Menuetto
f
p
f
p
8
Cl.
Cl.
f
p
f
p
cres.
f
15
Trio
Fin
sempre
23
sempre
31
f
p
f
p
39
f
p
f
p
44
cres.

Duet 2

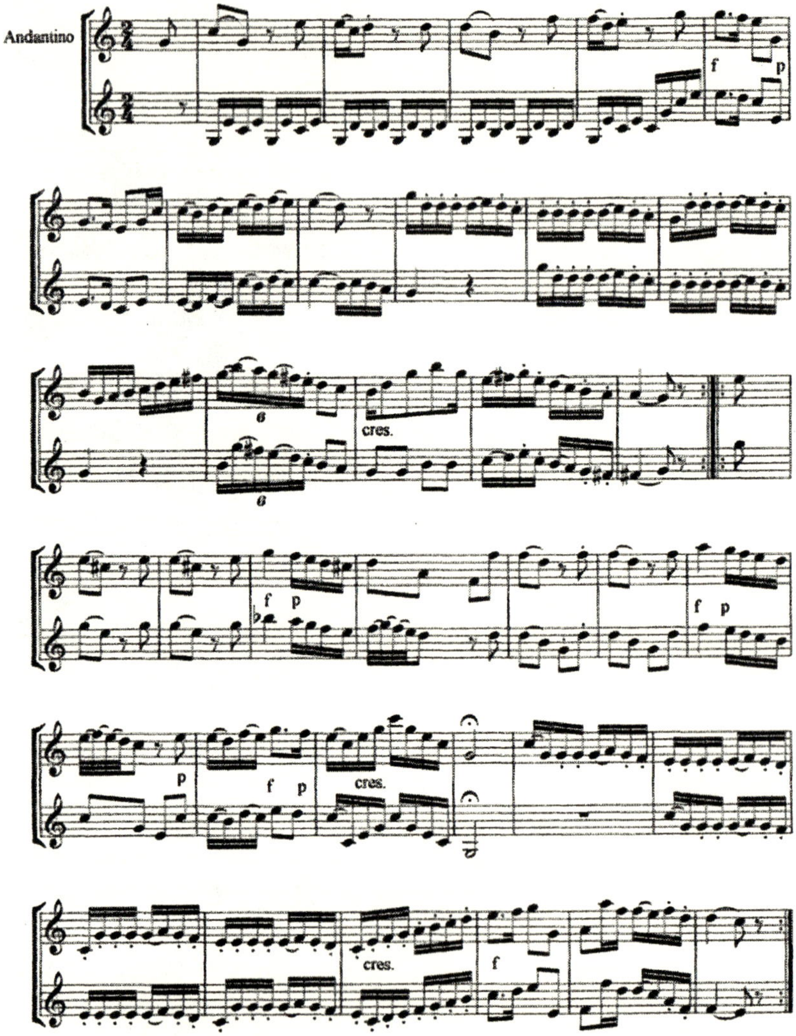
Andantino
f
p
cres.
6
f
p
cres.
f
p
p
f
p
cres.
cres.
f

Duet 3

76

Allegretto

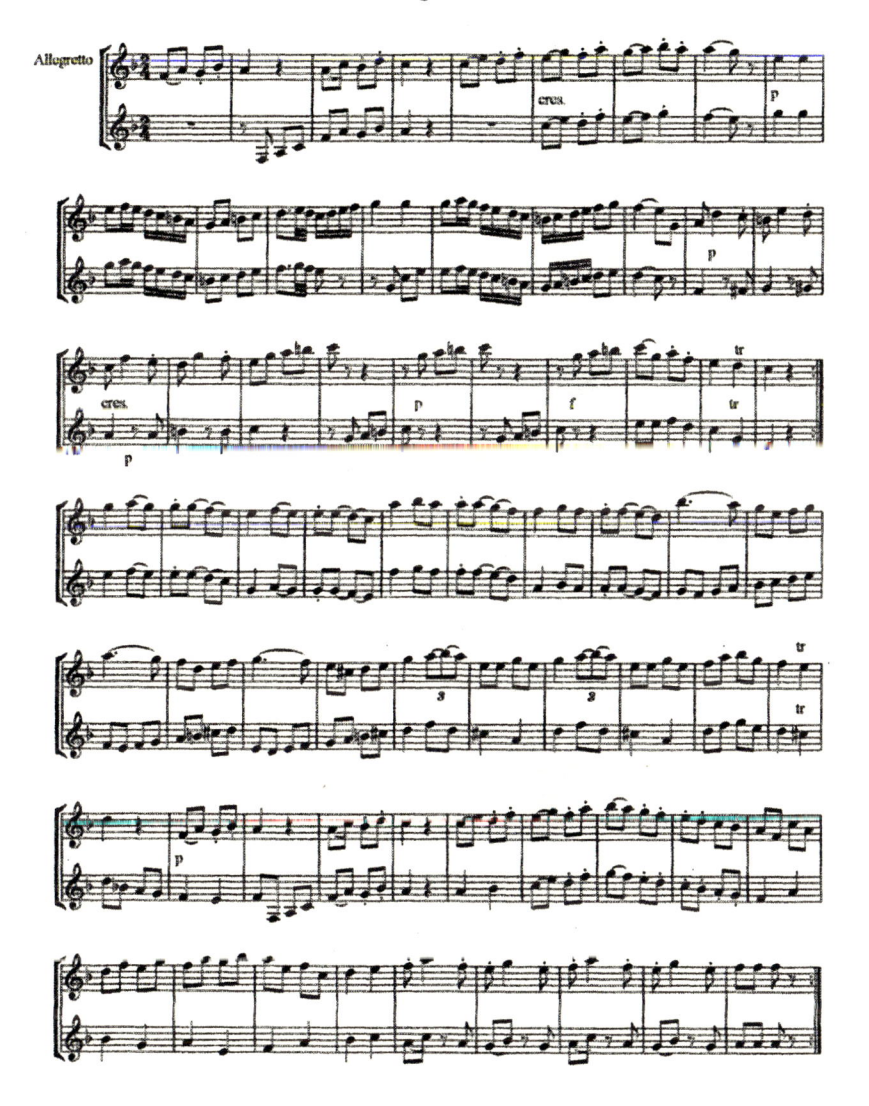

78

Duet 4

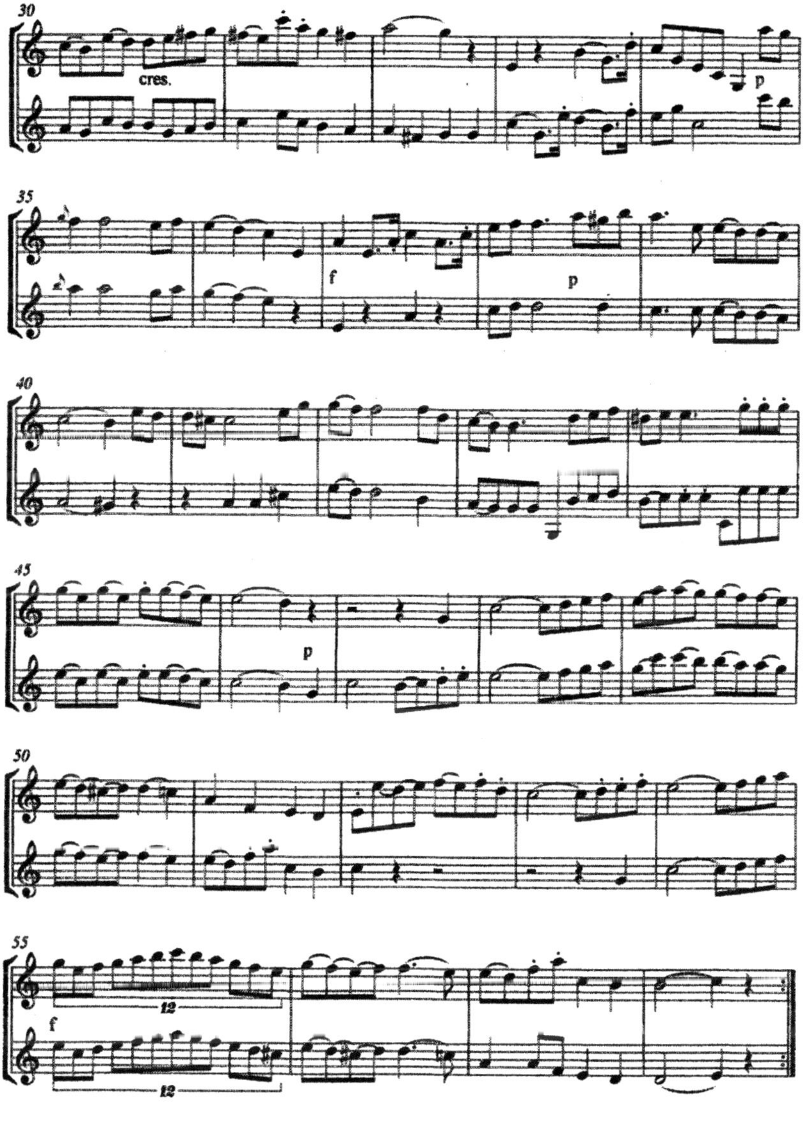
30
cres.
p
35
f
p
40
45
p
50
55
f
12
12

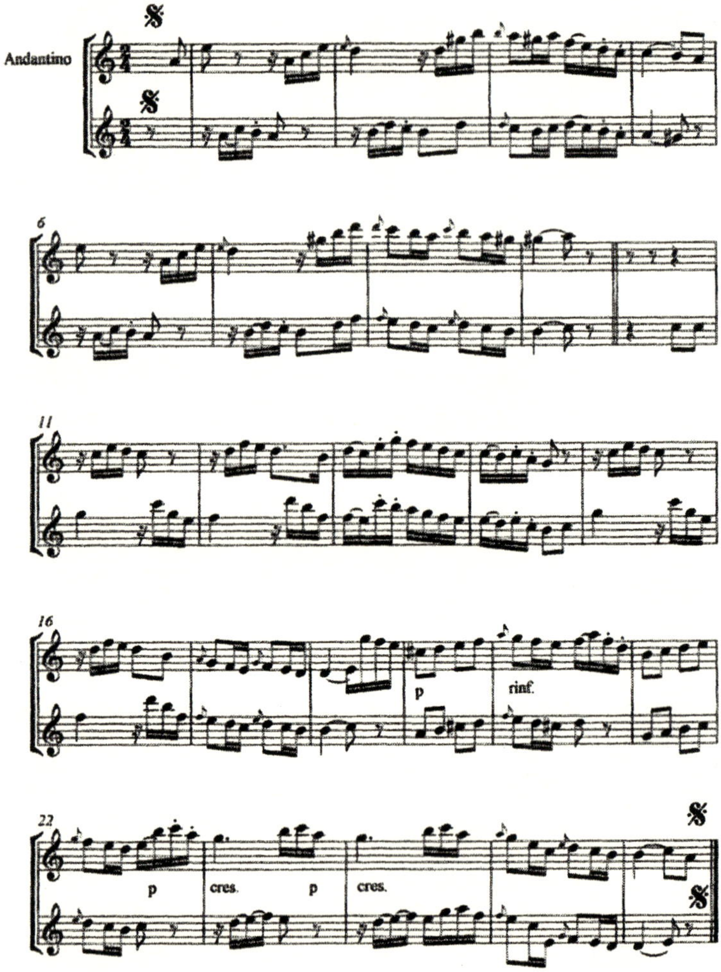
Andantino
6
11
16
p
rinf.
22
p
cres.
p
cres.

81

Duet 5

83

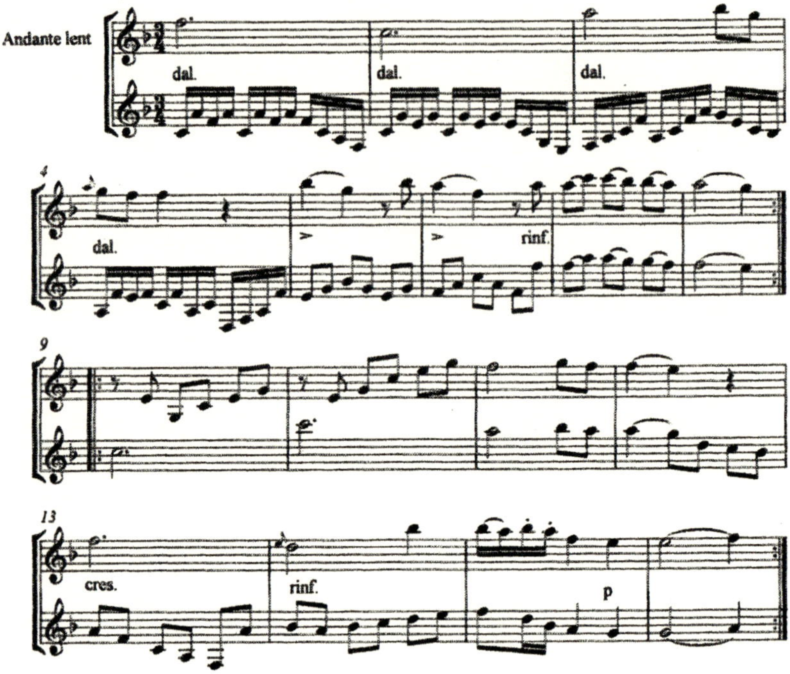
Andante lent
dal.
dal.
dal.
4
dal.
rinf.
9
13
cres.
rinf.
p

85

Duet 6

87

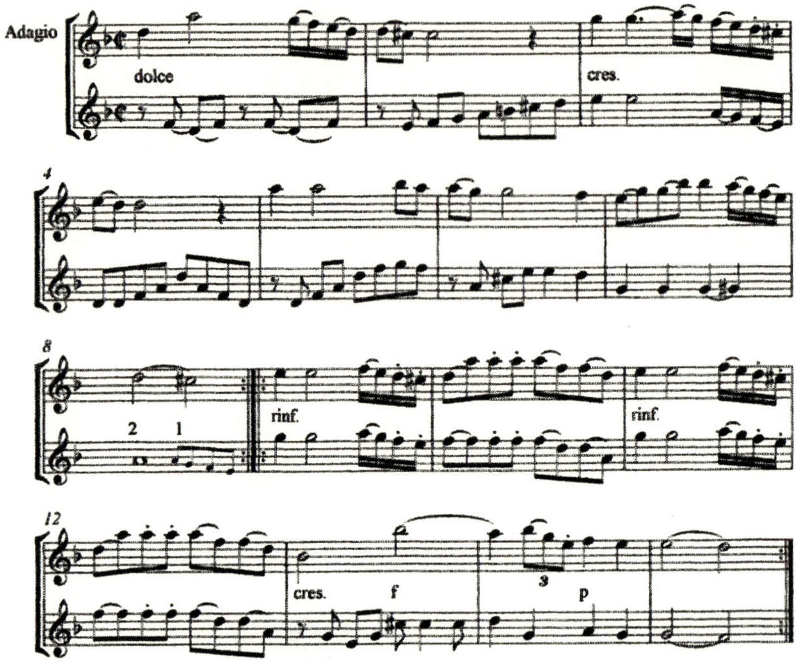
Adagio
dolce
cres.
4
8
2 1
rinf.
rinf.
12
cres.
f
3
p

89

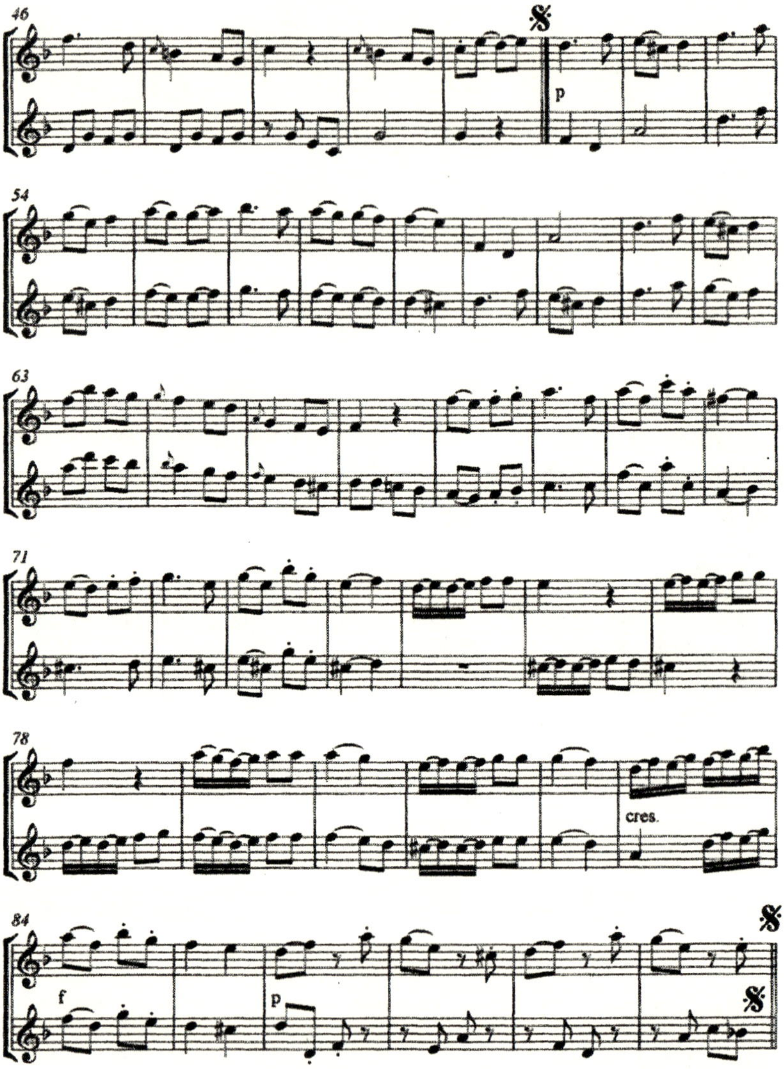
46
p
54
63
71
78
cres.
84
f
p

91

Now that this teacher can be usurped by your playing of this work, I will return to my pieces of which the two preceding are very difficult. Thus, in the duos of M. Michel [Yost][108] that you will find everything that is possible to do on the clarinet.

---

[108] Michel Yost (1754–1786) was a fellow clarinetist, Mason, and Guards' member of Vanderhagen.

Chapter 3
Nouvelle méthode de clarinette (1799)

Nouvelle MÉTHODE De Clarinette

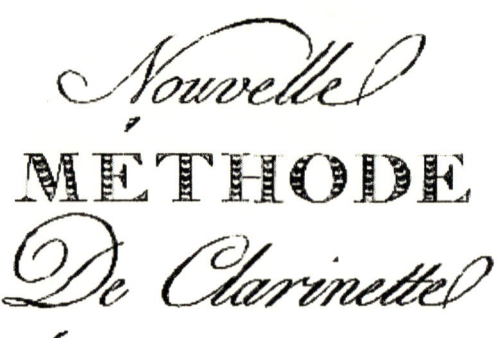

DIVISÉE EN DEUX PARTIES

Contenant tous les principes concernant cet Instrument ainsi que les principes de la Musique, détaillés avec précision et clarté.

Par Amand VANDERHAGEN

Professeur de Musique et Auteur de plusieurs Ouvrages pour Cet Instrument

Prix 15.

A Paris chez Pleyel Auteur rue Neuve des petits Champs N° 728
entre les rues Helvetius et Richelieu
Gravé par la C.*ne* Marie.

Reprinted, by permission of the BnF, from Vanderhagen, *Nouvelle methode de clarinette* (1799), title page.

A New Method for Clarinet, Divided into Two Parts
Containing all principles concerning this instrument as well as the principles of music, detailed with precision and clarity.

By Amand Vanderhagen, professor of music and author of several works for this instrument

Price: 15 livres

Published in Paris by the author Pleyel, rue Neuve on the petits Champs, No. 728, between the rues Helvetius and Richelieu
Engraved by C^{nes} Marie.

Observation of the Author on this Second Publication

I believe that it is very rare that the same author has published two methods for the same instrument, but for two reasons I have decided to do so. The first is the favorable reception that amateurs have deigned to give to my first treatise though it is very short. Second, it has been my desire to make it better. I believe I am obligated further to offer this one to the public as a more perfect and more detailed work containing not only all the principles of the instrument, but also all the elements of music.

I believe that I am also obligated to make beginners able to understand what I want to teach them, what a second [interval], a third, a fourth, a fifth, etc. are and, eventually, whatever enters into the first principles of composition.

I boldly hope then that the students of the fine arts and even the masters who teach them how to play the instrument with which we are concerned here, will be grateful for the care that I have used to perfect this work.

96

Natural Scale– Explanation of the Scale[109]

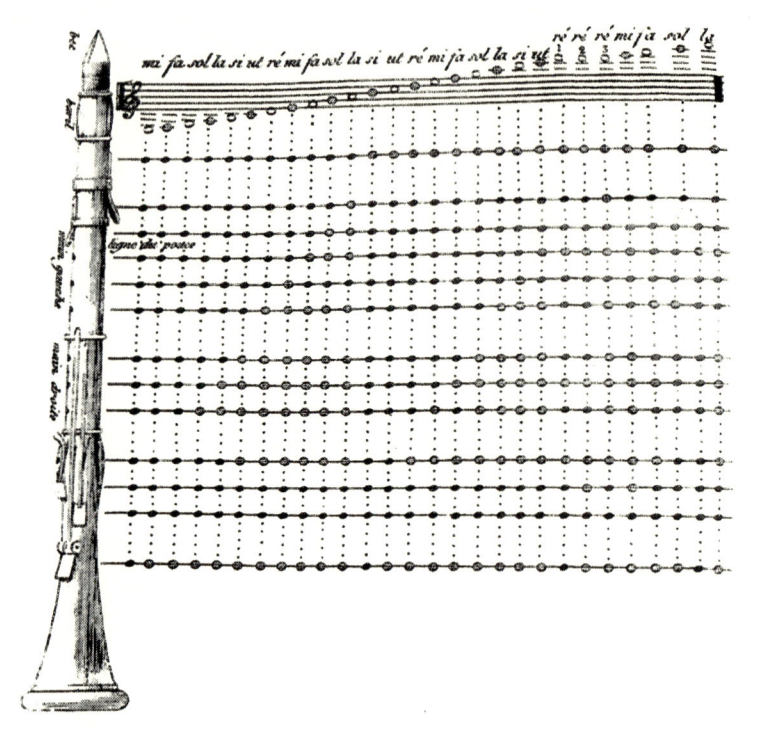

Reprinted, by permission of the BnF, from Vanderhagen, *Nouvelle methode de clarinette* (1799), 2.

All the transverse lines correspond to the holes and to the keys of the instrument. The black dots indicate the holes that must be closed, and the whites indicate the holes that must be open. But for learning the scale well, it is necessary to have an exact knowledge of the use of each key and of the sound that it produces. It is necessary to learn these keys in the following order by beginning with the three that are positioned on the stock-bell.[110] The first is the largest and makes the E of the bass and B♮ of the middle (E/B key). The second is the middle

---

[109] I have translated *Gamut* as "scale."

[110] I have translated *pavillon* as stock-bell, which is the swollen area of wood that is now referred to as a bell.

that makes F♯ in the bass and E♭ in the middle (F♯/C♯ key). The two other keys[111] close to the barrel make the small A of the second octave (A key) and the other, by gripping only without the teeth, with the thumbhole makes A♭ (register key).[112] But this same key is also useful because it is continually in motion. This produces the sound that suddenly makes the heavy sounds of the bass of the instrument or the clear sounds of the middle and high registers heard.[113]

As for the three different positions used to play the high D, certain clarinetists render it well by using the key of E♭. The others render the middle with the large key but the position marked No. 3 is good only as long as the D only passes in a rapid movement as in the following passages.

- All of the Ds above can be done with the A key:

---

[111] I have translated *placés* as "keys"; its literal translation is "places."

[112] Vanderhagen provides slightly different fingerings for the enharmonic notes of G♯ and A♭. G♯ is played by depressing the register key alone, while A♭ is played with the A key and the left thumb hole down.

[113] Refers to the register key.

98

Scale on the Sharps and Flats

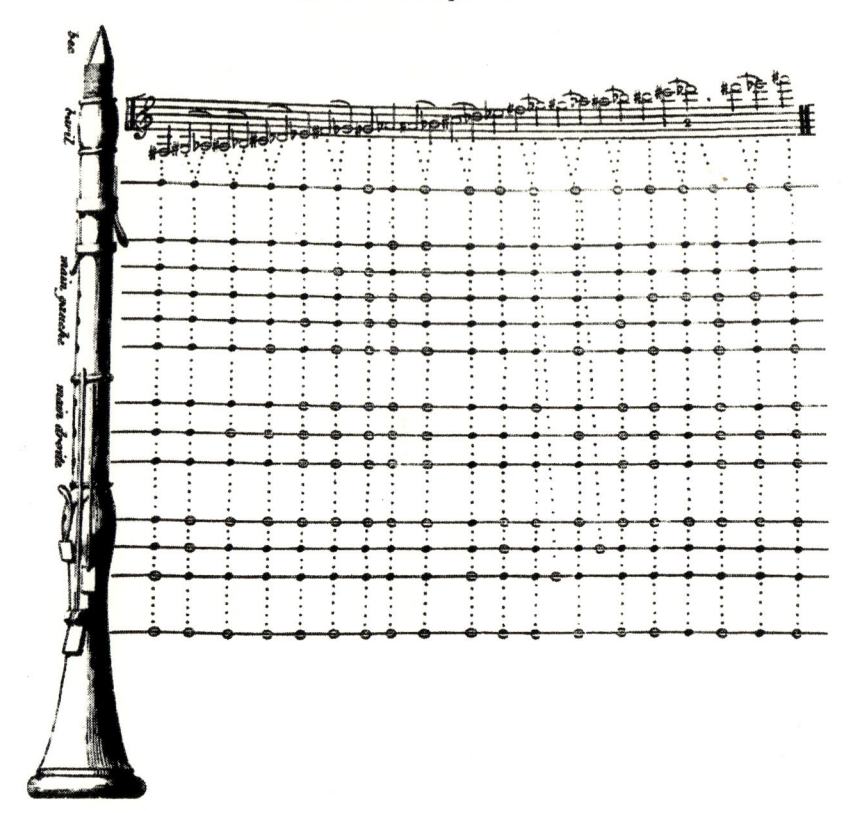

Reprinted, by permission of the BnF, from Vanderhagen, *Nouvelle methode de clarinette* (1799), 3.

Observation

There are two different positions for making high C-sharp. The first [position] that affects the C-sharps in this scale is marked by numbers. 1) The second is marked D-flat, and 2) the first is more equitable and able to sustain itself. But we are obliged to use the second option in difficult or rapid passages because it will be nearly impossible to produce with the usual fingering for C. See below.

99

Advice for Beginners

Read with the greatest attention all of the sections of this work. It is essential to understand them well and in order for each one to lead to the execution of the principles in it. Be well advised that without principles, there is no foundation at all and consequently no solid execution.

Therefore, follow carefully the principles that you have gone through. Let yourself be guided by the teacher who earns your confidence and learn all of them if you want to learn music. Do not torment him to let you play songs from opera or other popular melodies much too soon, for I know from a very long experience the weakness of beginning on this subject. But to what will they lead you? To a routine and not at all to music. So follow the principles. I cannot stress enough that this route will appear to take you on the longest, even the most boring path, but you will be delayed only to be convinced and even persuaded that this is the shortest and the most solid.

On the Position of the Body, the Arms, and the Head–A Preliminary Observation

You may reproach me for beginning here with the instrument instead of beginning with the first principles of music, but this is my method of teaching and my response. When I accept a student for the clarinet or for the flute and they know absolutely nothing, I begin by asking them to make an embouchure on the instrument and by giving them the positions indicated here below, without telling them of any musical notes in order not to divide their attention and because they find themselves quickly fatigued by maintaining their body position or by the

100

excessive quantity of air that they are using. I then make them quit the instrument to show them the notes and the other principles alternately with the instrument, and thus we pass in that way from one principle to another. I seek to spare them the inescapable boredom of the first lessons. I will now return to my subject.

In order to play any instrument whatsoever, it is necessary to handle it with grace, for when we play with grace we are certainly not constrained in any manner of execution. It also has the double advantage of nicely pleasing both the eyes and the ears. For playing the clarinet then, it is necessary to have an agreeable deportment. Hold the body straight as well as the head, which must never tilt towards the chest for this constricts the freedom to breathe. The two elbows are elevated without affection so that the bell of the clarinet is nearly a foot and half from the body.[114] The fingers are aligned over the holes without having any contact between the two hands, which must naturally follow the contour of the instrument.[115] The right thumb serves as support and the left thumb controls two objects by holding the thumbhole and the register key at the same time.[116] We sometimes use the embouchure to hold [the clarinet] without using the key, and it is for this reason that it must never be opened too much. It is the same for the movement of the fingers in general, for they must always raise themselves above the holes remaining perpendicular and at a very short distance above each hole. By raising them too high we risk not reconnecting precisely to the hole when lowering them, and furthermore this constrains its execution.

The small finger of the left hand has two keys to govern and must always be raised up for touching the one or the other as needed, and this happens very

---

[114] I have translated *pavillon* as bell because in holding the clarinet the distance of elevation is traditionally measured from the body to the bell.

[115] It is unclear what Vanderhagen means by *la pente de l'instrument*; he could be referring to having the fingers of each hand gently bent to fit the curvature of the clarinet or to how the hands will stretch to cover their sets of holes, respectively.

[116] I have translated *le trou à boucher* as "thumbhole," and *la clef* as "register key," because these are the two areas of the clarinet that are controlled by the left thumb.

often throughout the key of B. Guard yourself well then against contracting bad habits for they will be too difficult to break and will result in constraining you.

Embouchure

Here is another essential point that merits careful attention. The clarinet is not a difficult instrument up to a certain point, but it is also not one of the easiest when we want to attain a certain degree of perfection. That is impossible to obtain if we do not have a good embouchure, which is synonymous with a good sound. It is for this that the student must work from the beginning, for the embouchure is the basis of all wind instruments. It is not necessary therefore to push too much of the clarinet mouthpiece into the mouth, but only up to the shoulder of the reed, for by inserting it so far that your lips come up to the ligature you will have no other means of controlling it except by pinching which can be good only on the flexible part of the reed. We must not, consequently, have an embouchure around the reed except as I have said above, by supporting it on the teeth and covering the reed by the upper lip so that the teeth do not touch it at all. Being covered by the lip the teeth give strength for pinching or for modifying playing.[117] It is also necessary to take care that the two sides of the mouth are closed tightly so that we do not hear wind exiting from the two sides of the embouchure.

In beginning the scale in the bass, it is necessary only to contain the reed without pinching. We begin by not pinching only up to the note C, but we really pinch up to the high notes by resealing the lip gradually. We will observe the same process in a reverse direction in descending. Loosening the reed gradually, but always keeping it contained, prevents certain disagreeable squeaks that result from pinching too much or loosening the lips too much. You must not begin too soon with a reed that is too hard because your lips are not yet able to form an embouchure. You would be unable to continue and would fatigue

---

[117] In the eighteenth-century embouchure, the reed was most often placed under the upper lip and a double lip embouchure utilized.

considerably without ever creating the pleasant sound of the instrument. It is not necessary meanwhile that the reed be too soft, for you would then produce only very weak or even very disagreeable sounds and would hamper progress. You must search for a good compromise by taking a very strong reed and weakening it because it is very easy to perfect its fit by shaving it a little with a penknife.

The First Lesson on the Instrument: An Observation

I have placed here two fragments of the scale of which the one is in the bass of the clarinet and the other in the middle. I believe that I am obliged to take this position because I have found that beginning students can produce C, , more easily than F or E of the bass. For this reason it will be good to begin with C, but it will always be preferable, in my opinion, to begin in the bass, because the two thumbs, as well as the fingers, are employed which gives a certain aplomb for holding the instrument.[118] Thus, after having lightly traveled through the following three examples and acquired some knowledge of the principles of music, we will pass through the different scales that follow. As for articles 6, 7, 8, and 9, it is necessary to wait until your knowledge is a bit advanced before studying them.

- Example 1: Sustain the reed without pinching.

---

[118] Engraver mistake: *mais* should be *pouce*.

103

- Example 2: Loosen the lips and sustain the reed.

- Example 3: Equally good.

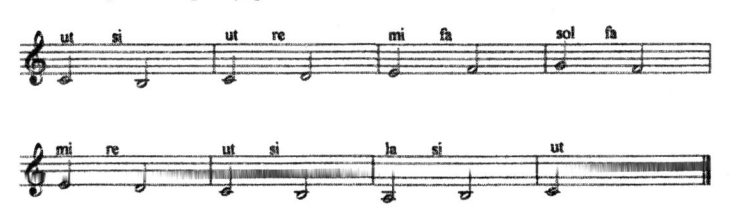

Principles of Music on the Knowledge of Notes

In order to learn the notes promptly, it is necessary to begin by learning the five lines by heart and the notes that are placed on it, and next the spaces, so that you will pass through those that are found placed below and above the five lines. You should examine their figure as well as the quantity of lines through which they pass at the top and bottom. Here they are:

Between the lines

- The first note at the bottom of the five lines is D.

- The first at the top of the five lines is G.

- Bass notes which are also called chalumeau.

- High notes.

When you have a complete knowledge of all these notes, not sequentially by the diatonics as we say of C, D, E, F, G, A, B, C, but by their construction, and you will know how to name them indiscriminately without order and without sequence by passing from a bass note to a high note and taking them in sequence in the middle. At last when you are doubtful neither of their name nor of their appearance, it will be necessary to work on their positions in order to make each note of the instrument sound. This is the duty of the instructor who teaches you. I have placed the scales at the head of this work where all the positions are demonstrated, but they are absolutely there only to guide your memory pending the absence of the teacher and to help you to recall the positions that you may have forgotten.

105

Different Scales

These different scales, as much by conjunct motion as those by disjunct motion, are exercises for preparing the fingers that the student will need in the course of this work. Conjunct motion uses several notes that follow each other without leaps, like the examples below. Disjunct motion is a set of notes that leave between each a vacant place like C, D, E, and F as you will see in the following.[119]

Connected Steps

- No. 4 All of these scales do not need to be measured, as it is a matter only of sustaining the sound in order to learn the keys.

- No. 5

- No. 6

---

[119] Fux's *Gradus ad parnassum* (1725) states that conjunct lines refer to motion by step and disjunct lines feature motion by leaps.

- No. 7

- No. 8 Sustain the sound well, and pinch gradually in ascending; diminish the same way when descending.

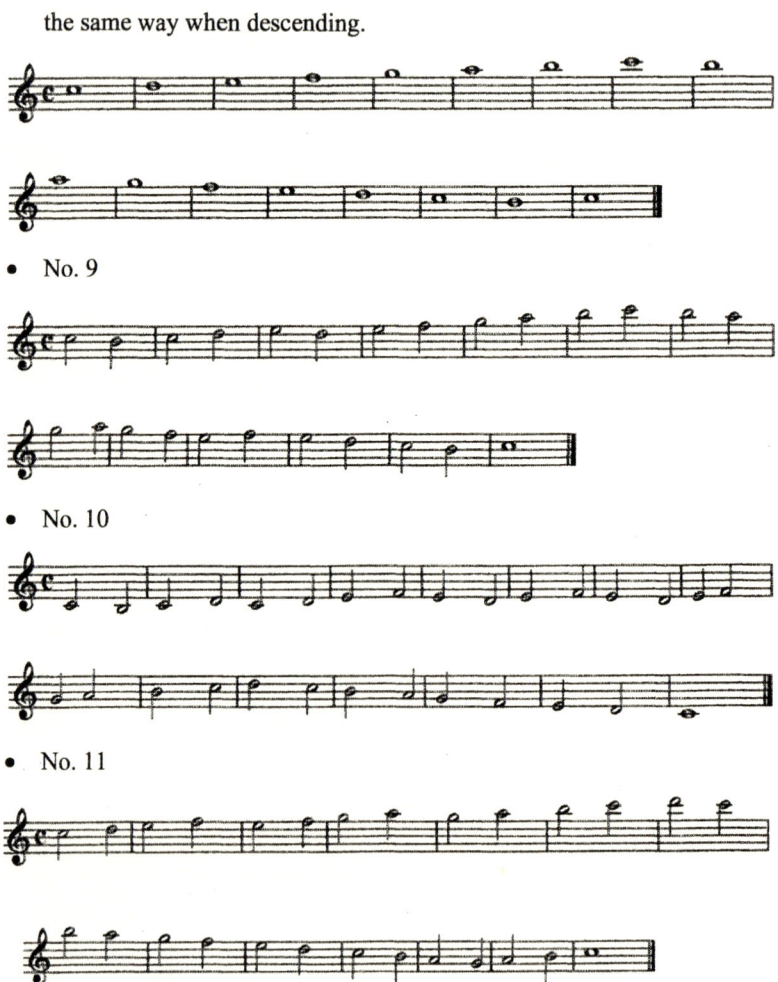

- No. 9

- No. 10

- No. 11

- No. 12

Observation

As we are not always able to exhale, it is understood that this is fatiguing, especially in the beginning. In order to rest, we must then understand the principles below, which are followed again by the other scales proper for forming fingerings.

Introduction
Article 1- Concerning All the Signs of Which Music is Composed
Know the five lines that are counted in ascending [order]:

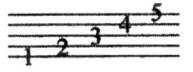

The clef is placed at the beginning of the five staves and serves to make known the nature of the instrument or the voice. There are only three clefs in music. Know the clef of G, the clef of F, and the clef of C, but there are different styles of their placement.

The clef of G is placed on the first and on the second lines but we use only the one placed on the second line.

- Not used   We use only this one

There are also two F clefs that are placed on the third and on the fourth lines, but we use only the one placed on the fourth line.

- Not used   We use only this one

There are four C clefs and they serve everything. We place them on the first, the second, third, and fourth lines.

Seven notes: C, D, E, F, G, A, B

Seven values to know: whole note, half note, quarter note, eighth note, sixteenth note, thirty-second note, and sixty-fourth note.[120]

The dot that serves to augment the note by half of its value.[121]

Measures are formed by the small lines, which perpendicularly cross the five lines.[122] The time signatures indicate the beats of the measure.[123]

Measures in four beats   Of two beats   Barred to also be played in two beats

Of two quarter beats   Of three beats   Of three quarters similar to three beats

Derived by three, and by three quarters   Derived by four beats   Derived by two beats

---

[120] I have translated *ronde* as "whole note," *blanche* as "half note," *noire* as "quarter note," *croche* as "eighth note," *double croche* as "sixteenth note," *triple croche* as "thirty-second note," and *quatriple croche* as "sixty-fourth note."

[121] *Le point*, "the dot," refers to a dotted note.

[122] Word omitted, reconstruction mine.

[123] Word omitted, reconstruction mine.

In all of these different measures, there are only two that are truly fundamental. Know that those of four beats form an equal measure and those of three beats form an unequal or limping measure, as they contain only the three quarters of the first measure. Beyond this we can consider all of the others only as divisable by the first two.

The Rests: Know the whole-note rest, the half-note rest, the quarter-note rest, the eighth-note rest, the sixteenth-note rest, and the sharp, the flat, and the natural, which are also the three accidental signs.[124] There are, moreover, many other signs that are explained in the following articles.

---

[124] I have translated *pause* as "whole-note rest," *demi pause* as "half-note rest," *soupir* as "quarter-note rest," *demi soupir* as "eighth-note rest," and *quart de soupir* as "sixteenth-note rest."

Article 2: Of the Value and the Shape of Notes

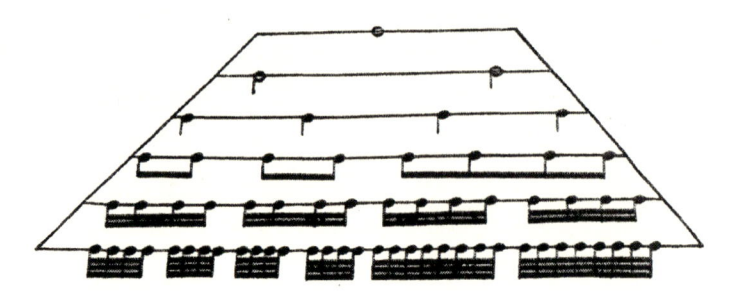

Whole note
Half notes
Quarter notes
Eighth notes
Sixteenth notes
Thirty-second notes

One whole note
worth 2 half notes
or 4 quarter notes
or 8 eighth notes
or 16 sixteenth notes
or 32 thirty-second notes

Reprinted, by permission of the BnF, from Vanderhagen, *Nouvelle methode de clarinette* (1799), 12.

One half note – worth 2 quarter notes – or 4 eighth notes – or 8 sixteenth notes – or 16 thirty-second notes – or 32 sixty-fourth notes

Reprinted, by permission of the BnF, from Vanderhagen, *Nouvelle methode de clarinette* (1799), 12.

111

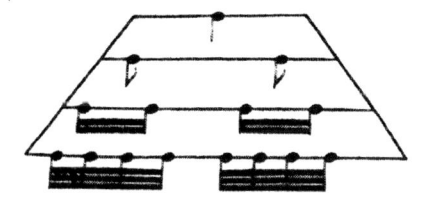

One quarter note – worth 2 eighth notes – or 4 sixteenth notes – or 8 thirty-second notes

Reprinted, by permission of the BnF, from Vanderhagen, *Nouvelle methode de clarinette* (1799), 13.

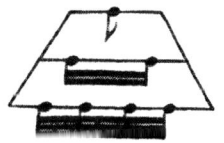

One eighth note – worth 2 sixteenth notes – or 4 thirty-second notes

Reprinted, by permission of the BnF, from Vanderhagen, *Nouvelle methode de clarinette* (1799), 13.

One sixteenth note – worth 2 thirty-second notes

Reprinted, by permission of the BnF, from Vanderhagen, *Nouvelle methode de clarinette* (1799), 13.

Article 3

What is the value of a dotted note? The dot augments the note that precedes it by half of its value. See the example below.

This example shows the name and value of the rests, and therefore of their relationship with the notes.

The small dots that are leading from the first to the second line indicate the effect and the value of the dot, of its name, and of the value of the rests, as well as their relationship with the notes.

Explanation

A rest can mean the silence of an entire measure. We often blend together several of them. The half-note rest is the silence of one half measure of four beats because it replaces the values of two quarter notes.

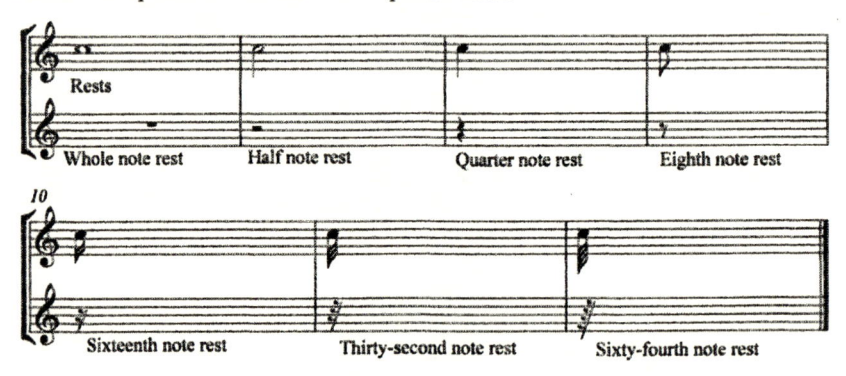

Several Combined Rests[125]

We can combine together several silences of several measures by means of a sign which we call the breve and the half breve. The breve occupies from the fourth to the second lines in descending and represents four measures, and the half breve occupies only two lines and represents two measures.

- Example[126]:

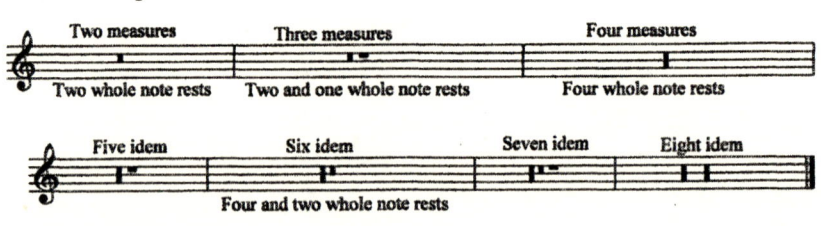

---

[125] I have translated *reunis* as "combined."

[126] I have translated *baton* as "4 whole-note rests" based on Vanderhagen's musical illustration.

Article 4

For sharps and flats, their position determines their effect in the same way as for the natural. The sharps raise the note a half pitch, the flat lowers the note a half pitch, and the natural returns the sharped or flatted note to natural pitch. Sharps are arranged by fifths in ascending and flats are arranged by fifths in descending or by a fourth in rising.

- Sharps: F double sharp, ♯, or ✕ or else ; a double sharp forms a natural pitch. For example, an F♮ doubly sharped becomes a G like a G-double sharp will become an A.

- Flats: double flat ♭♭ ; a double flat also forms a natural pitch. For example, an E♮ made doubly flat becomes D like a B-double flat becomes an A.

Observation

The sharps and flats serve not only to raise and lower the notes but also to indicate the key in which we want to play. Their ordered placement is such that they are indicated by the figures of which I have spoken. For example, in a key where it would be necessary only to sharp the clef, the sharp can be placed only on the F. If there are two, it is on F and C; if three, F, C, and G, and so on. The same order is observed for the flats— for this see the beginning of Article 6.

Accidental Signs

There are three accidental signs–know the sharp, the flat, and the natural, but they are considered to be accidentals only when they are not part of the key and when they are found by accident in the middle of a piece of music in supplementing the sharps and flats with which the key contains. See the following example.

Effect of a Sharp and a Flat and of the Flat and the Natural

- Natural note: the same raised a half pitch because of the sharp, the same lowered a half pitch and returned to its natural sound by means of the natural.

- Natural note: the same lowered a half pitch because of the flat, the same raised a half pitch and returned to its natural pitch because of the natural.

Here you clearly see in the example above that the natural causes two different effects: it lowers the sharpened note and raises the flatted note.

Article 5: Sequence of Signs

The following signs are all as necessary to know as those which are contained in the preceding articles.

The return sign: 𝄋 This sign is ordinarily placed at the beginning of a section of music that is played in a rondeau and at the end of each reprise as well. Every time you encounter this sign, you must always return to the opening.

Da capo: When this word is placed at the end you must return to the beginning as with the reprise sign. The simple small lines are the measures and the double lines, when there are points of reprise, indicate that each reprise must be played two times. There are some pieces where four reprises can be found and some times more, and then even more returns. This demands more attention than the others because it is found among all the reprises. Other types of reprises, which do not repeat at all because there are no points in the interior, can also be distinguished by two double bars but these have points only on one side. See the following.

repeat — without repeat — repeat — repeat — without repeat

- Sign for slurring the notes.

- For detaching the notes.

- Signs for increasing and diminishing the volume.

116

Article 6: On the Number of Sharps Which Are Necessary in Each Key, and to Relative Keys[127]

We say that a pitch is relative to another pitch when it is designated in the key by the same number of sharps or flats.[128] See the following.

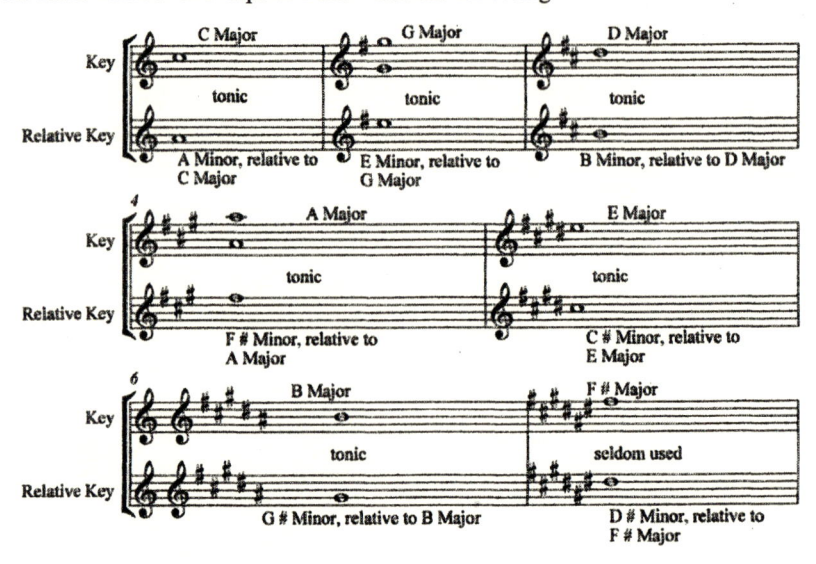

---

[127] I have translated *ton* here as "key."

[128] Here I have translated *ton* as "pitch."

Like the Preceding
Exceptionally here there is a question of flatted pitches.

Observation on Article 6: For Knowing the Tonic Note

The tonic note is the nominative note of the key of the piece in which you will play.[129] All of the notes of the scale, when taken separately, are essentially tonic notes because with them you can play in C, in D, in E, in F, in G, in A, and in B.

The tonic note of each mode, major or minor, for there are only two modes, can be recognized in the major tones by the sharps because it follows the last ascending sharp note. For example, in G there is only one sharp in the key and it is placed on the F, for it then makes G the tonic. In D we have two sharps in the key, F and C, which makes D the tonic note. See the preceding examples: each note is a tonic.

---

[129] I have translated *ton* here as "key."

With the sharps in the minor mode it is precisely the opposite of what we have just said, because here the tonic is found a pitch below the last indicated sharp. For example, in E minor there is only one sharp on the F, which makes E, the pitch below it, the tonic. In B minor it is F and C that make B the tonic note, and so on.

In the major keys with flats the marking is different for the tonic is found four notes or degrees below the last flat given or five degrees if we count the note which carries the last flat. Regard the key of F above.

In the minor keys with flats the tonic is found a third above the last flat given. Regard the tone of D minor. In the following example you will learn that this is called a triad.

Article: On the Scale

It is not sufficient to know the scale by its ordinary denominations of C, D, E, F, G, A, B, C, for we must also know that these eight notes form the eight scale degrees. See No.1 below.

It is necessary then to know that these eight notes do not form eight tones but rather only five whole tones and two half tones. See No. 2 below. You will also get to know the other function of the notes of the scale in terms of composition which we will not refer to as C and E but instead as a triad. Here is No. 3. In the eighth article you will learn what composes a triad and therefore the other chords.

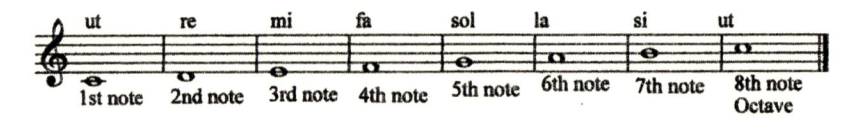

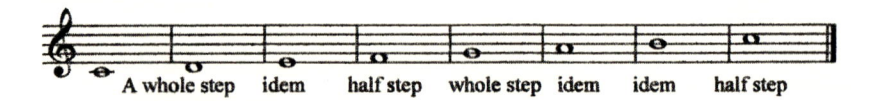

[Musical staff showing scale degrees: Tonic, Second, Third, Fourth, Fifth, Sixth, Seventh, Eighth]

Observation: The leading tone is always that which precedes the tone to a single degree of distance.[130] Here the seventh is always major, even in the minor mode.

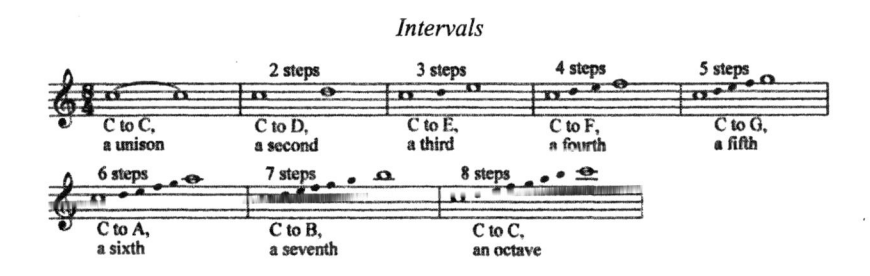

Intervals

[Musical staff showing intervals:]
C to C, a unison
C to D, a second (2 steps)
C to E, a third (3 steps)
C to F, a fourth (4 steps)
C to G, a fifth (5 steps)
C to A, a sixth (6 steps)
C to B, a seventh (7 steps)
C to C, an octave (8 steps)

Of Inversions[131]

Inverting an interval changes the ordinary placement of notes that form the chords. For example, C and D, like those above, are a second, and this same D, when placed an octave lower in the bass as in the following example, becomes a seventh and so on.

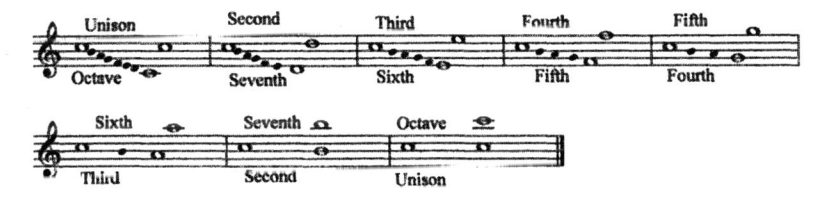

[Musical staff showing inversions:]
Unison / Octave
Second / Seventh
Third / Sixth
Fourth / Fifth
Fifth / Fourth
Sixth / Third
Seventh / Second
Octave / Unison

---

[130] I have translated *la note sensible* as "leading tone"; its literal translation is "sensitive note."

[131] I have translated *renversement* as "inversion," referring to interval inversions; its literal translation is "reverse."

Reason for the Function of the Notes Above

Someone might ask you why we call a note or interval a unison, second, third, or fourth, and the response is very simple. We call two notes that are on the same degree, when there is no distance between them, a unison. A second occurs when there are two degrees like C and D, and because we must always begin with the first interval, C to E, three degrees, and the fourth, C to F, four degrees, and so on. See the example of intervals.

Article 8: What the Intervals are Composed of[132]

A minor second is composed of a half tone

A major second of a tone

An augmented second of a tone and a half

A diminished third of two half tones

A minor third of a tone and a half

A major third of two tones

A diminished fourth of a tone and two half tones

A perfect fourth of two tones and a half tone

An augmented fourth of three tones and two half tones

A diminished fifth of two tones and two half tones

A perfect fifth of three tones and a half tone

An augmented fifth of three tones and two half tones

A minor sixth of three tones and two half tones

A major sixth of four tones and a half tone

An augmented sixth of four tones and two half tones

A diminished seventh of three tones and three half tones

A minor seventh of four tones and two half tones

A major seventh of five tones and two half tones

An octave of five tones and two half tones

This interval does not change

---

[132] I have translated *les distances* as "intervals."

121

Article 9: Instruction on What All of the Inverted Intervals of Minor and Major, and the Augmented and Diminished Intervals, Become

Instruction: the writing above each line announces the subject and forms the question and the writing below each line forms the response. The small notes that descend towards the bass note are scale steps.[133] For example, what if we ask you what an inverted minor second becomes? Here, for the first question on the first line, the response is a major seventh, and so on.

What becomes a minor second?	A major second	An augmented second
A major seventh	A minor seventh	A diminished seventh
A diminished third	A minor third	A major third
An augmented sixth	A major sixth	A minor sixth
A diminished fourth	A perfect fourth	An augmented fourth or tritone
An augmented fifth	A perfect fifth	A false fifth or diminished fourth
A false diminished fifth	A perfect fifth	An augmented fifth
An augmented fourth or tritone	A perfect fourth	A diminished fourth
A minor sixth	A major sixth	An augmented sixth
A major third	A minor third	A diminished third
A diminished seventh	A minor seventh	A major seventh
An augmented second	A major second	A minor second

Article 10: Definitions of Italian Terms that are used for Indicating Tempos and Expressive Markings

Largo – this is the slowest of all tempos

Larghetto – a little less slow than *Largo*

---

[133] I have translated *les petits points* as "small notes"; its literal translation is "small points."

Adagio – calmly and less slow than *Largo*

Grave – less slow than *Adagio* with a certain gravity in its execution

Affectuoso – between *Andante* and *Adagio* with an affectionate and sweet expression in song

Amoroso – tenderly, moves sweetly and slowly

Andante – light: this is a tempo that responds to graciousness

Andantino – less lively than *Andante*

Moderato – moderately

Gratioso – graciously

Allegro – lively

Allegretto – less lively than *Allegro*

Vivace – quick

Presto – lively

Prestissimo – very lively; this is the fastest of all the tempos

Cantabile – freely singing and without forcing

Dolce – sweet

Piano – soft, it is marked by p[134]

Pianissimo – very soft, *pp*

Mezzo forte – play at half strength

Mezzo voce – at half voice

Forte – strong, it is marked by *f*

Fortissimo – very strong, by two *ff*

Sotto voce – singing at half voice, or playing at half strength

Rinforzando – to swell the sound suddenly, it is marked *rinf*

Crescendo – to swell the sound gradually, it is marked *cres.*

Smorzando – to let the sound die, *morz*

Sostenuto – sustaining the sound

Rinforte – between strong and sweet, *rinf* or *rf*

Solo – alone

---

[134] I have translated *doux* as "soft"; its literal translation is "sweet" or "gentle."

Da capo – returning to the beginning of the piece

Article 11: The Measure

The measure is one of the basic principles of music, exactly dividing the notes it produces without the need to be conducted, and its beating furnishes the proof of the value of each note or rest to be observed exactly.

The measure is so necessary in execution that by altering it too much we make even the most well known melody unrecognizable. Focusing all of your attention to this principle is essential, and be persuaded that to play poorly but in time is preferable to divine playing where no tempo is observed.

For the vocal part, we are taught to beat time with the hand, but for the instrumental part the hands are occupied, and so we tap with the end of the toe. But, for counting well, we should avoid large movements for they entrap the body and ruin aplomb.

For counting a measure of four beats we mark the first beat with the end of the foot and the second and third beats are marked internally by the big toe of the foot. This is what we call beating the measure in the shoe. The fourth beat is marked by raising the tip of the foot, but when we play in an orchestra all the beats are counted internally as only the conductor is permitted an obvious beat.

The measure of two beats is much easier to count as we must only put the foot down on the first beat and raise it on the second.

With three beats mark the first externally, mark the second internally, and raise the foot on the third.[135]

I have indicated the place where we can begin to beat the measure. In order not to divide our attention for this exercise, I use only diatonic scales prepared for this purpose.

---

[135] Word omitted in original, reconstruction mine.

Article 12: On Breathing

This article is also most essential for those who want to play a wind instrument, for we do not always find a named point of silence or a rest when we need to breathe. In retaking a breath we can do it only by shortening the value of a note. It is good then to know in what circumstances we can breathe without altering the musical phrase, and what notes are susceptible to being reduced a little, along with those where we must avoid breathing. For example, on the tone leading to the tonic note we can never breathe here, ,but rather we must breathe after the tonic, as we can not breathe on any slur that connects several notes. As you see clearly here by this example, , if you breathe between the first and second notes the slur will be interrupted. When you breathe after the second note it is then marked by the abbreviation *res:*, which the slur makes, and thus the intention of the composer is met despite the second note having part of its value reduced.

You have still other circumstances where you are able to breathe easily, such as on the half phrases and musical phrases where we ordinarily re-encounter these at the fourth or eighth measure, for example:

Notice carefully the second and third measures of this example where one quarter note is marked by an accent on the top and two others slurred. In all similar circumstances, you will always be able to breathe before the first note.

I will finish this article with an opinion on breathing in general. Many students exhale until they have a total deficiency of breath, which causes them to breathe poorly, and very often in the very middle of a very interesting phrase, which it disfigures. For this reason we must never wait until this extremity and breathe wherever it is possible. By these means we are less fatigued and thus perform better.

Disjunct Degrees

In the first dozen scales, we have always marked conjunct degrees, and now we are going to make another mark and run through the instrument by disjunct degrees and in the different tones and modes. But I am going to begin by demonstrating the rapport that exists between the fingerings of the bass of the clarinet and those of the upper register. That is to say, up to C there are no other changes of position from low to high except for the movement of the thumb of the left hand, which stops the thumbhole while releasing the register key for making the bass and closes the thumbhole by pressing the register key to obtain the middle and the high registers in such a way that the E of the bass and the B on the third line use the same fingering.[136]

Example[137]:

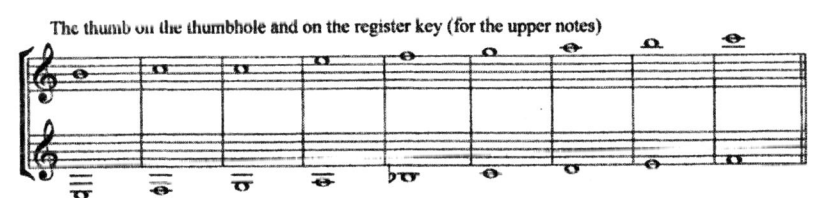

---

[136] I have translated *lachant* as "releasing" and *la clef* as "register key."

[137] I have translated *le trou* as "thumbhole."

- Movement by seconds

- By thirds

- By fourths

- By fifths

- By sixths

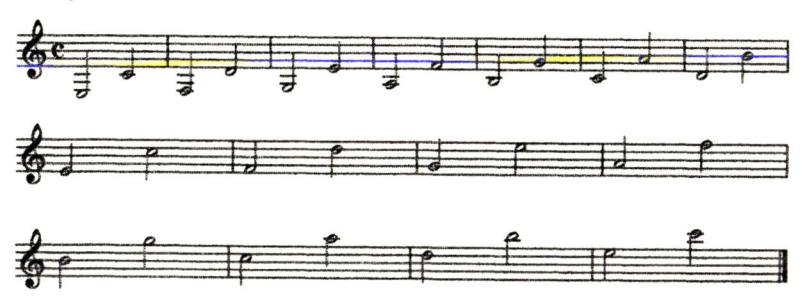

- By sevenths

- By the octave

- By tenths

- By the double octave

Lesson

- Another

- Another

- Another

- Another

- Another in F

- Another

- Another

- In D minor

- Another

131

Examples of Chromatics

This lesson is most essential for familiarizing ourselves with sharp accidentals, which we often find in the course of a piece of music.

Same Example for Flats

Observation

Now that we have succeeded up to here, it is supposed that we have acquired a perfect knowledge of notes and fingerings; can we now begin to count measures? Observe how the foot must mark and beat the first note of each measure exactly after having sustained each note during the four beats.

- Whole Notes: *Lent*

- Another: Half notes

- Another: Quarter notes

- Another

- Another: Eighth notes

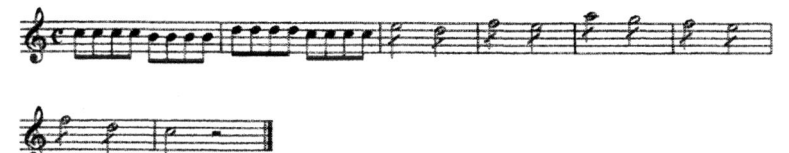

- Another

- Another in 2 beats

- Another

- Another

- Another

- Another in F

- Another in 2 quarter notes

- Another

- Another

- Another in 3 quarter notes

- Another, an inversion of the previous example

136

- Another

- Another, an inversion of the previous example

Note the similarity of these lessons to the two preceding, which proves that the three-eight measure is another choice for shortening measures of three-four [time] or three beats. Because each measure is able to contain only the value of the three eighth notes, it must count each eighth-note for a beat.

- In 3/8

- Another

- *Allegro*

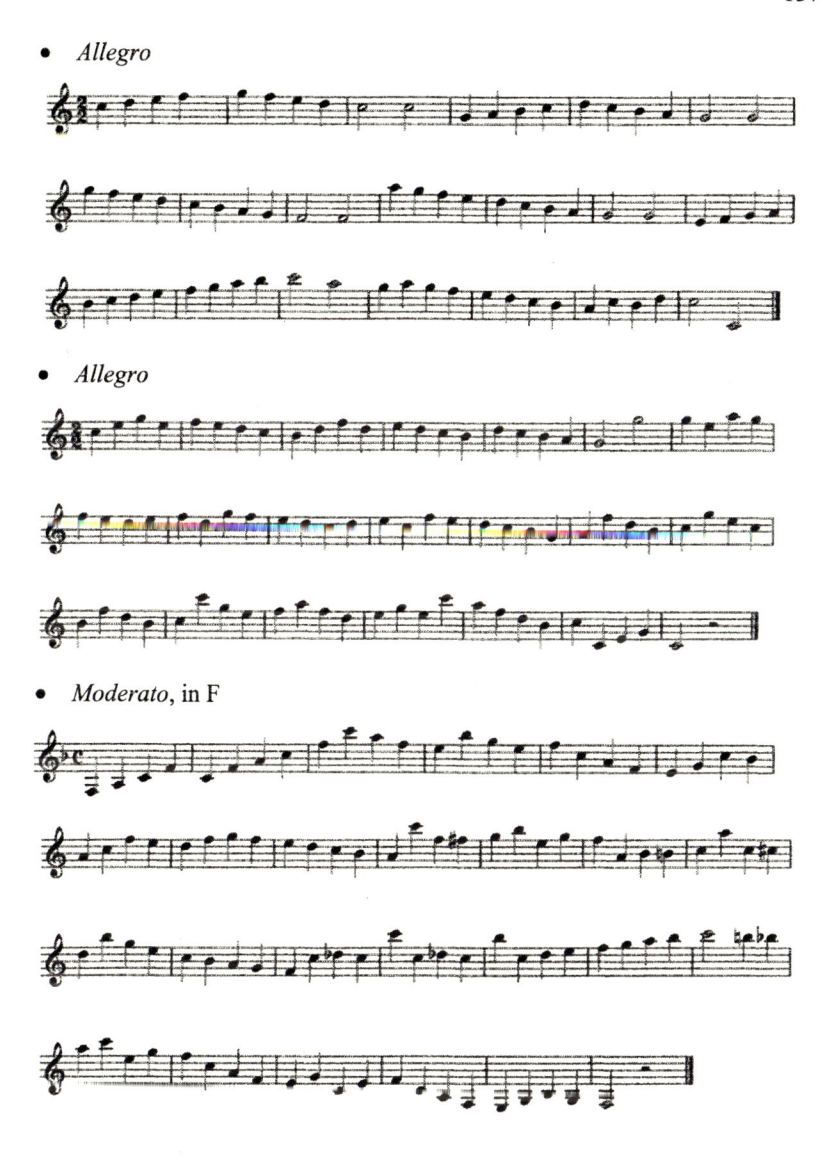

- *Allegro*

- *Moderato*, in F

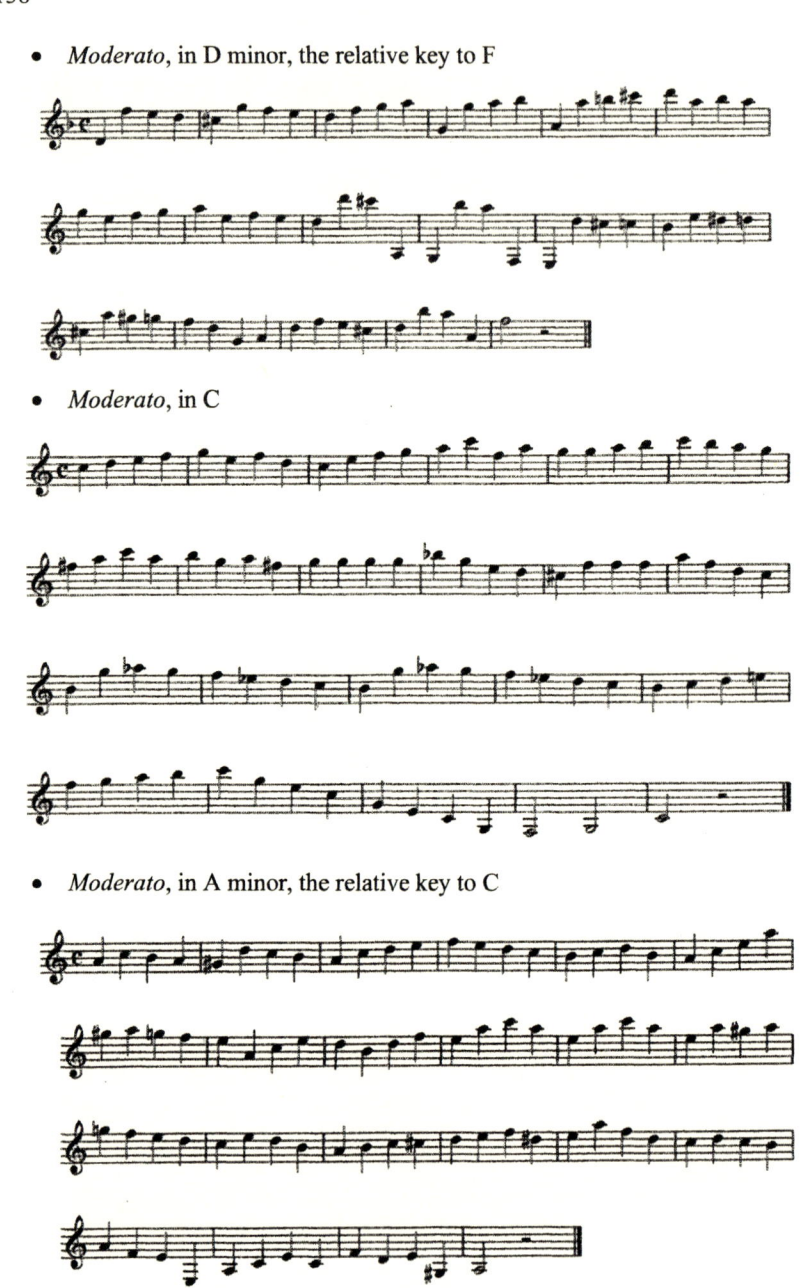

- *Moderato*, in D minor, the relative key to F

- *Moderato*, in C

- *Moderato*, in A minor, the relative key to C

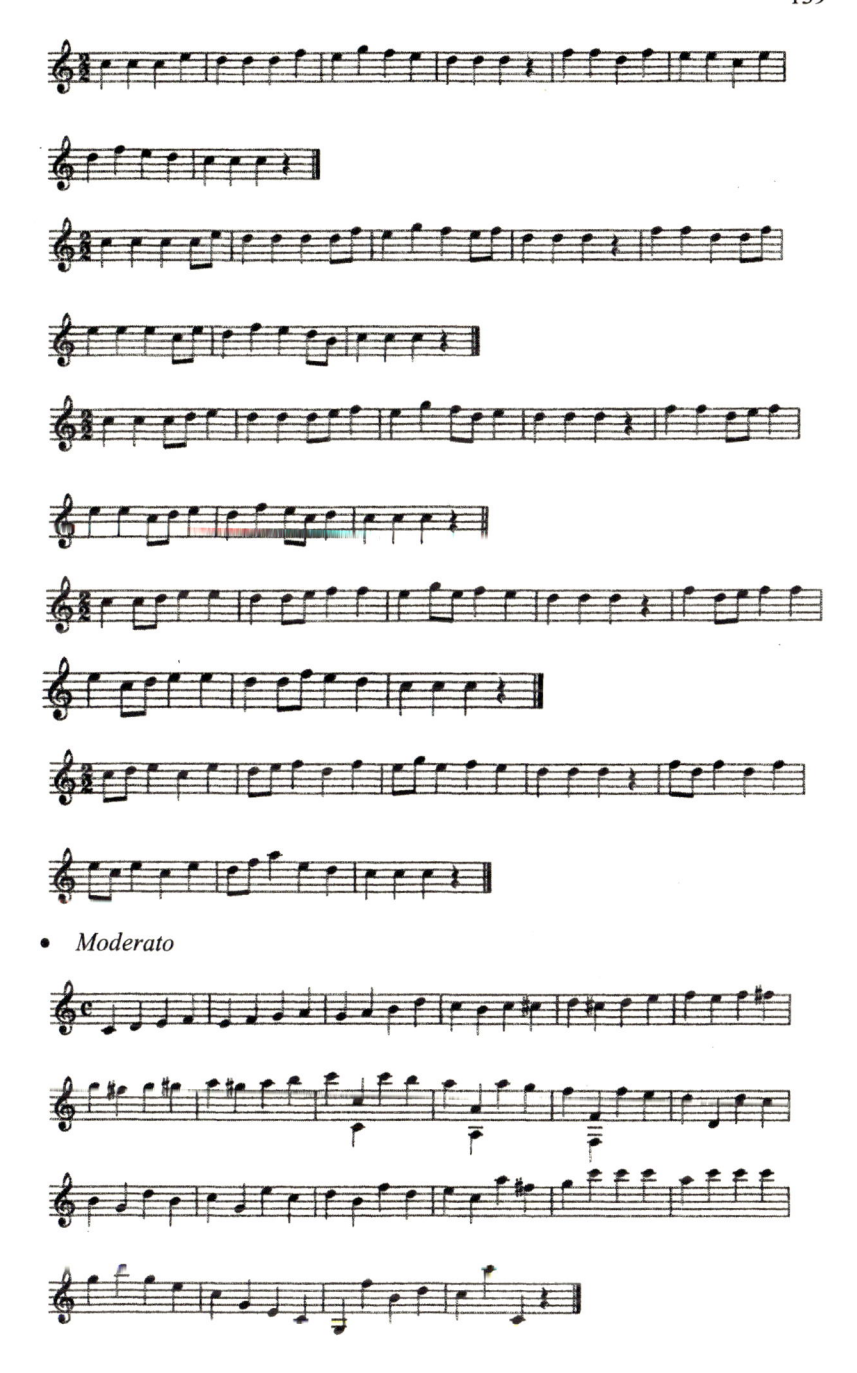

• *Moderato*

- Another

- Lesson for making ourselves familiar with the keys

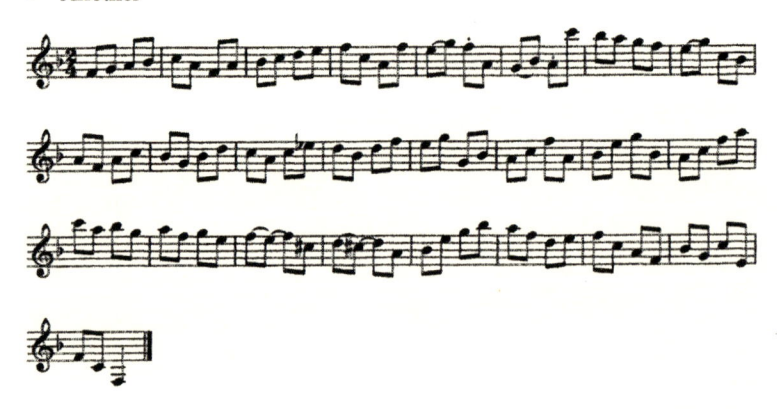

- Another

- *Moderato*, in B♭

- *Moderato*, in G minor, the relative key of B♭

- *Moderato*, in E♭

- *Moderato,* in C minor, the relative key of E♭

Lesson on the Bass Notes of the Clarinet

Many teachers neglect this part of the instrument, which is nonetheless most essential when playing a duo concertant where we play alternately the solo part and the accompanying part and where we follow the beats as you will see below. How then will we be able to ascend rapidly through all of these bass notes if we have not perfected our fingerings [?].

Examples

- *Allegro moderato*

- Another *Allegro*

- Another *Moderato*

- Another *Allegro*

- Another *Moderato*

Chalumeau

All that you have just seen in the preceding examples is precisely what is called the chalumeau. When we find the word chalumeau written under the notes, it means that these same notes are one octave lower. See below.

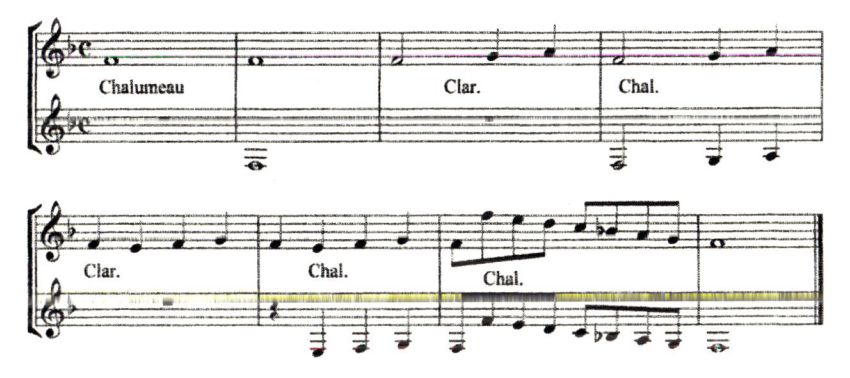

144

The Perfect Chord with Its Inversions

The perfect chord is composed of the tonic, the third, the fifth, and the octave, independent of the place that it holds in the composition. It serves to prepare the ear for the key in which we are going to play, which is often announced by one or several perfect chords. Here I have put only the perfect major chords expecting that they differ from the perfect minor chords only by the third that in the first case is major like C and E♮, and in the other like C and E♭.

- In C:

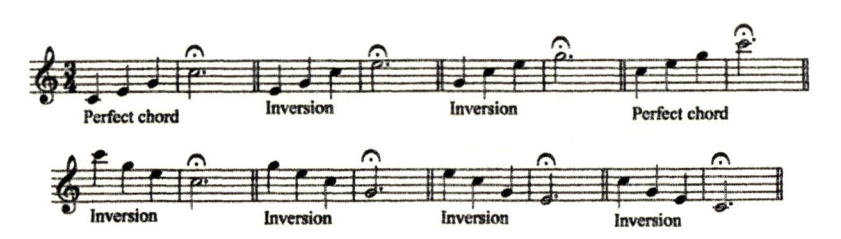

- In D:

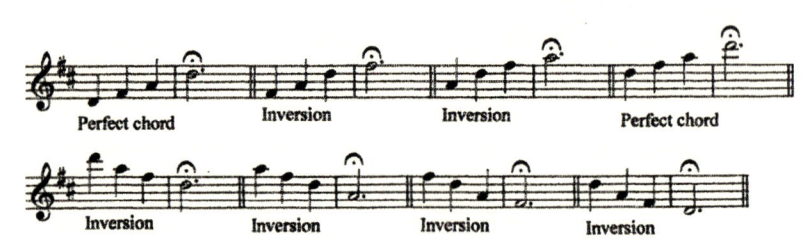

- In E:

- In F:

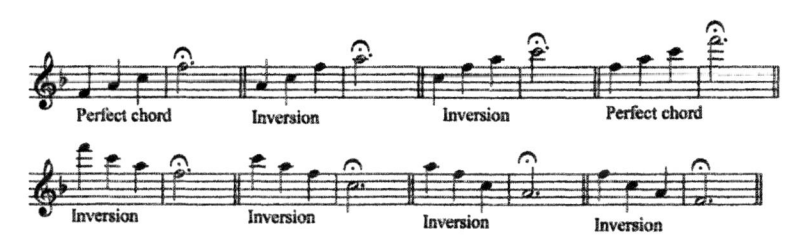

- In G:

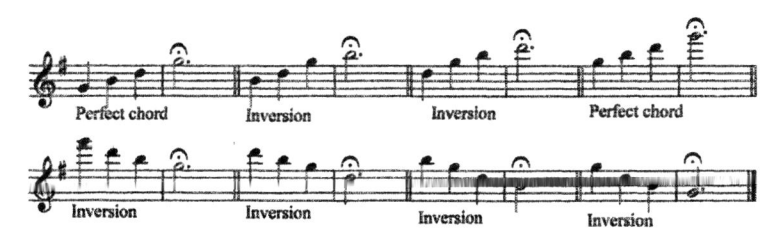

- In A:

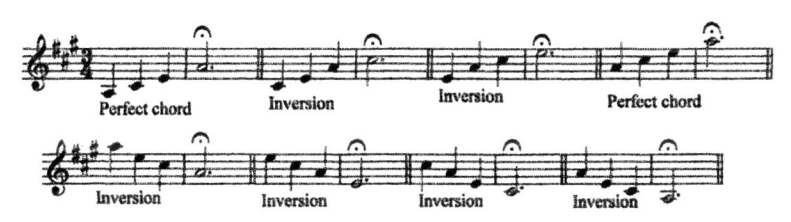

- In B♭:

Article 13: Of Tonguing and of the Slur[138]

There are different ways of giving articulation– know *legato* and *staccato*.[139] The first makes no interruption in the sound from one note to another for it connects several notes in the meantime without the slur, while the second detaches all of them. The first expresses itself by "Tuh" and the second by "Tee," and when slurred there is only a single manner of expression. It is done, more or less, by slurring the notes by two, three, four, or by a much greater number, but it is always slurred.

We cannot form a pleasant song without using articulation and slurs as they serve wind instruments precisely like bowing serves the violin, so apply yourself seriously to the study of it.

Examples

- No. 1, By a legato "tu"

- No. 2, By a staccato "te"

- No. 3

This one is the most beautiful and the most useful because the two last notes of each four is marked by dots. It is not necessary for these to be detached by a

---

[138] I have translated *coup de langue* as "articulations"; its literal translation is "strokes of the tongue."

[139] I have translated *möeleux* as "legato"; its literal translation is "mellow." I have translated *le sec* as "staccato"; its literal translation is "[a] dry [note]."

staccato stroke for we must use legato. The dots are there only to distinguish the articulations and slurs.

- No. 4

When the stroke begins with three notes, we must have four consecutive articulations of the type in the first measure, for it is only the fifth note that receives an articulation and similarly in the second.

- No. 5, The first is marked and the three others are slurred.

- No. 6, Articulation on the first and on the last of each four.

- No. 7, Slurring two-by-two; this articulation is most essential.

- This is the reverse of No. 5:

Observation

When we encounter a passage like the one above where there is no sign of slurs nor articulations, as it happens very often, it will be necessary, if the movement is *moderato*, to use the articulation as indicated in No. 3, and if it is an *Allegro* then as in No. 7, and if the movement is too fast as in No. 9.

- No. 3, *Moderé*: two slurs and two articulations

- No. 7, *Allegro*: slur two-by-two

- No. 9, Very fast, slur all

- Legato articulation by "tu"; three to a beat

- Articulation by "te"; as such but detached

- The first two slurred; it is the most useful articulation

- The last two slurred

149

- A bit difficult

- Slur three-by-three

- Marking the first [notes]

- Slur all six but the first must be distinguished by a stronger expression than the others

Recapitulation

For the following two examples, perform successfully all of the articulations indicated in Article 13.

First Example

150

Second Example: Legato, then Staccato

Article 14: Appoggiaturas and Other Grace Notes[140]

The appoggiatura is a little note following another on the same pitch and it carries the sound of the pitch above or below it.

Note: As a general rule, a small note always slurs onto the note that follows.

- Example: Appoggiaturas and their effect

Grace Notes

Grace notes are small notes which fill-in the intervals of the third like the following.

---

[140] I have translated *port du voix* as "appoggiaturas"; its literal translation is "carrying the voice." I have translated *notes de gout* as "grace notes"; its literal translation is "tasteful notes."

151

- Grace notes and their effect

Mixed Example of Appoggiaturas and Grace Notes

Appoggiaturas – Grace Notes – Appoggiaturas   Grace Notes – Appoggiaturas – Grace Notes – Appoggiaturas

Observation

The sign ~, which is placed sometimes after a dotted note, as we see on the line below, is executed as it is indicated by the small notes of the second line.

152

Observation on Grace Notes

We employ grace notes principally when we descend by thirds as I have described above. Moreover good taste often adds this embellishment! There are, however, cases where we must never add anything to the intervals. For example, in a tutti section of a large orchestra where all the instruments are an ascending or descending ensemble, like , and other similar cases we must play the note purely and simply, for grace notes can be practiced only in the phrases of song and when we are playing alone. Two instruments playing the same song separately can easily make their own particular sounds, but combining their different manners of feeling and expression would certainly create a very bad effect.

It is necessary then in similar cases to avoid what is called embellishment. That is to say, never add anything by itself and hold strictly to the note.

Article 15: The Trill and the Turn[141]

The trill is designated by *tr* or + and is formed by borrowing the note which is a step above it and which carries the sign of the trill, and it is completed by the note which is a step below it.

---

[141] I have translated *cadence* as "trill"; its literal translation is "sequence." I have translated *brisé* as "turn"; its literal translation is "broken."

In order to learn how to trill well you must begin by moving the finger slowly, and then with the same movement, you will increase speed gradually and finish with two small notes, which make the end of a trill more pleasant.

- Examples: trill on D for finishing on C

- On G for finishing in F

- On A for finishing in G

- On F for finishing on E♭

The Turn

The turn of two notes borrows one from above and one from below the principle note and is therefore designated by ~ ~ ~. See below:

154

Lesson on Dotted Notes

This measure is derived from four beats and forms a double 6/8.

- Dotted whole notes

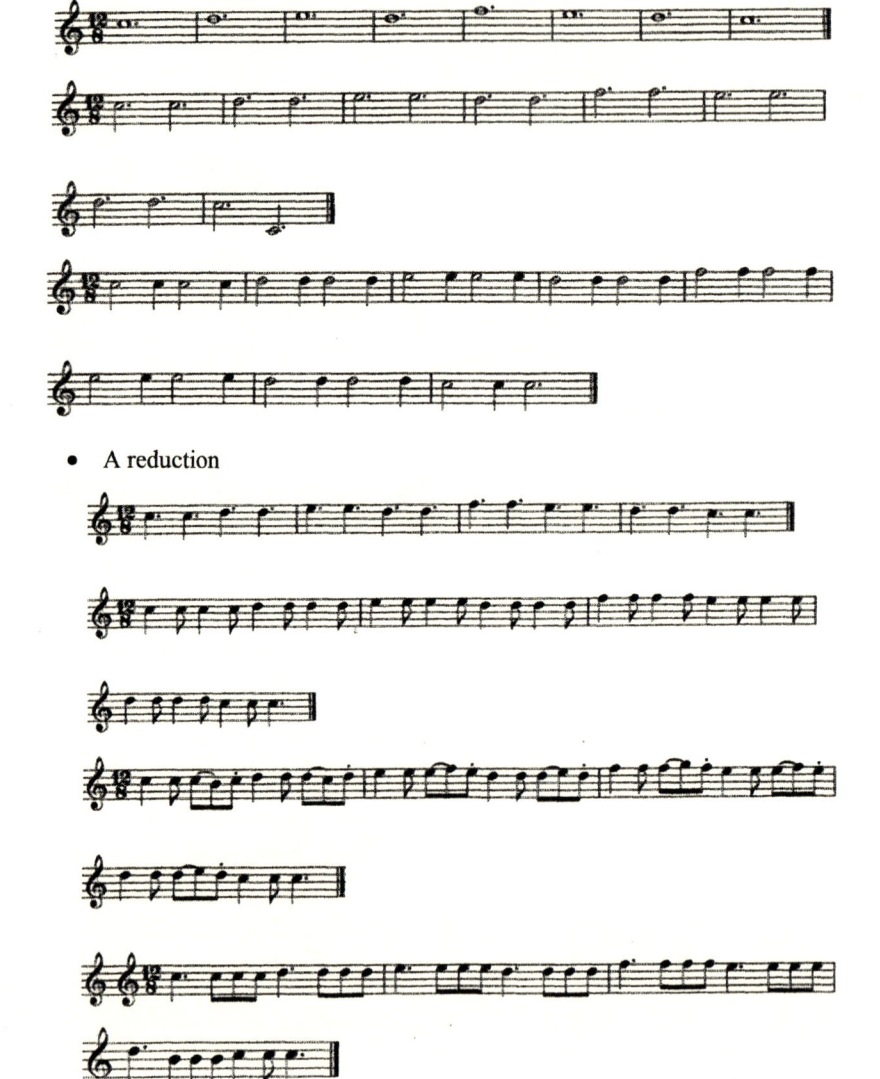

- A reduction

Lesson on Dotted Quarter Notes

- Value of the dot

156

- Another

- Dotted eighth notes

-
  Dotted eighth note

  Its value and effect

- Another

- Another

- Dotted hemiola and its effect

- Dotted half note, count in 3 quarter notes, and its value

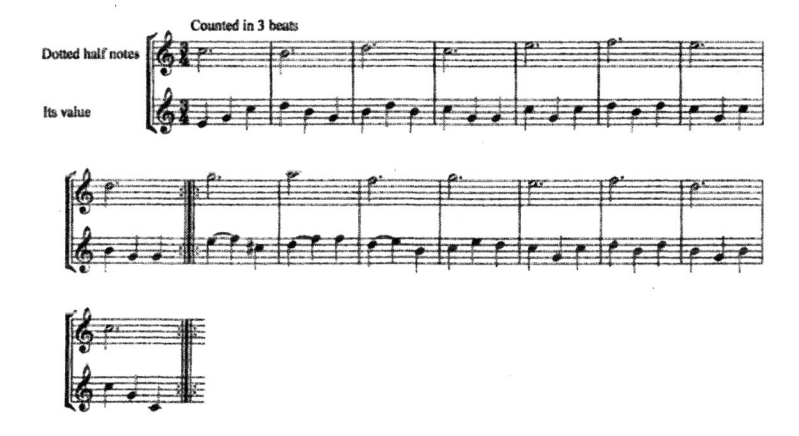

- Dotted quarter note

- Dotted eighth note

- A different marking

- Another

- Another

- Another

159

- Dotted double eighth notes, beat in 3/8

- Another

- Dotted quarter notes, beat in 6/8

- Another

- Another

- Another

- Another

Article 16: Lessons on Rests[142]

We cannot study this musical part too much for there are no pieces of music that do not contain rests. A single eighth-note rest poorly realized, when its time is forgotten, cripples an entire measure and can derail all the other parts if it is not addressed and overtaken promptly in the following measure. One or several measures are easy to count but the shorter the silence the more difficult it is to count with precision, so the best method then is to listen to the bass or another part of the accompaniment that fills the void made by the silence.

---

[142] I have translated *les silences* as "rests."

- Another

- Half rests

- Another

- Another

- With quarter note rests

- Another

- Another

- Quarter- and eighth-note rests

- Another

- Another

- Eighth-note rests

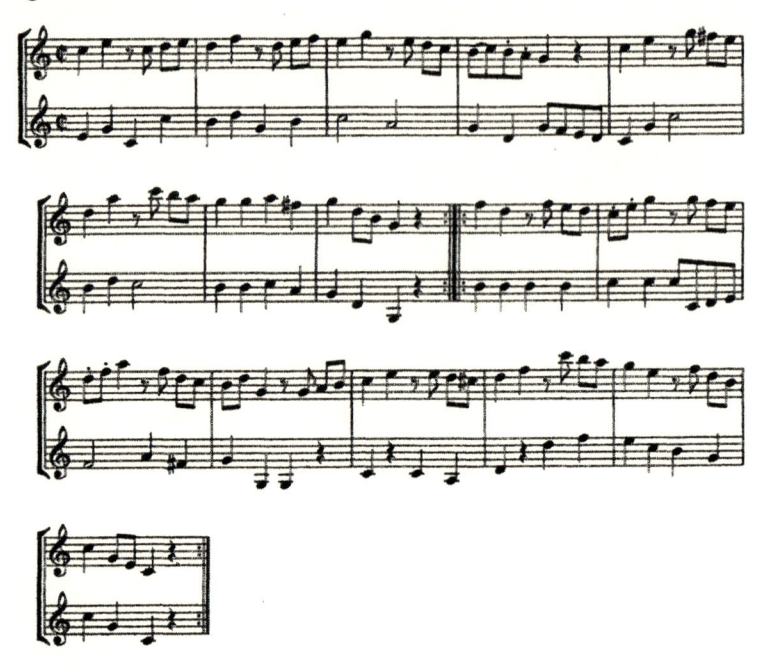

- Another

- Another

- Another

- Another

- Another, *Moderato*

- Another, *Moderato*

- Another

- Count in 3 quarter notes

- Another

- Another

- Another

- Another

- Another

Observation

As all of the following examples offer a different tempo with rests in each part, the student should play alternatively between the first and second parts.[143]

- The first line, the second is the reverse of the first; in 2 quarter notes

---

[143] I have translated *marche* as "tempo"; its literal translation is "pace" or "march."

- Another

- Another
- Another

- Another

- Another, *Andante*

- Another, *Andante*

- Another, *Andante*

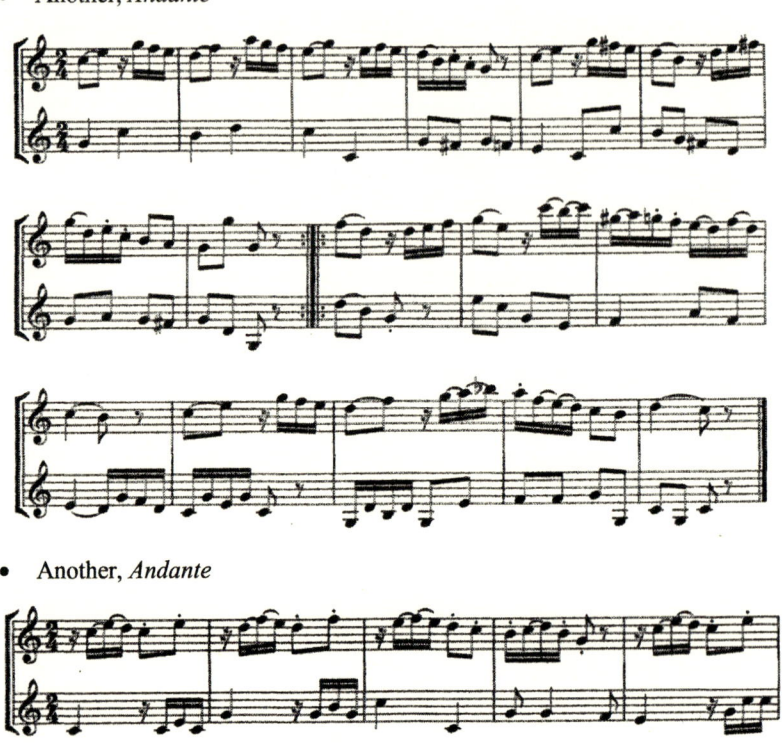

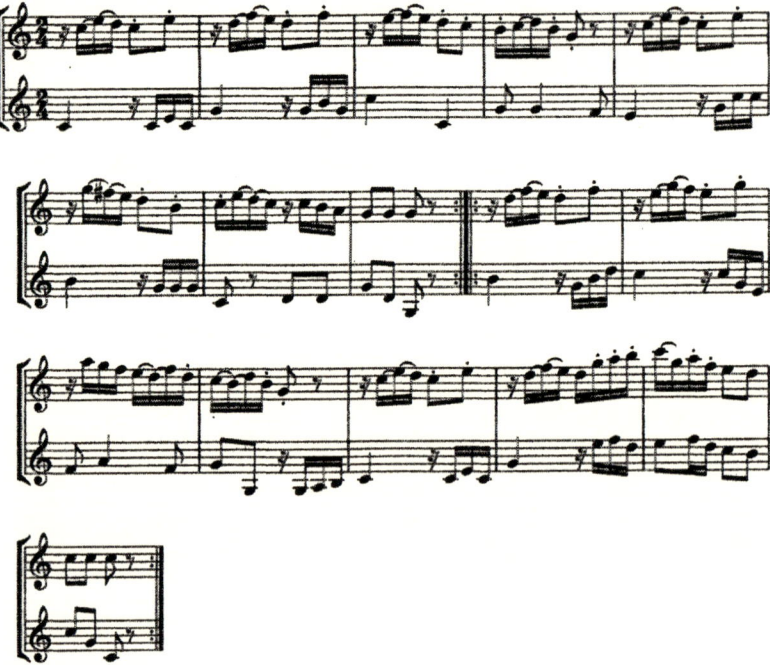

- Another

- Another

- Another

- In 6/8

- Another

- Another

- Another

- In 12/8

- Another

185

- Another

Article 17: On Syncopation

Syncopation is a long note between two short notes. In order to express it well we must give a staccato stroke on the note that precedes it.[144] See below.

---

[144] I have translated *un petit coup sec* as "staccato articulation"; its literal translation is "a short dry note."

- Another in F: the two slurs from one measure to another thus form the syncopation

- Another type of syncopation

- Another in A minor: eighth-note syncopations

187

- Another; syncopated quarter notes

- Marking syncopations in a measure of 2 quarter notes [2/4]

- Another

- Another, syncopated eighth notes

- In 3 quarter notes [3/4]; syncopated equal notes

- Another

- Another

- Another

- Another manner of designating the syncopation

- Another; Lesson on the equality of articulations

- Another

- Another

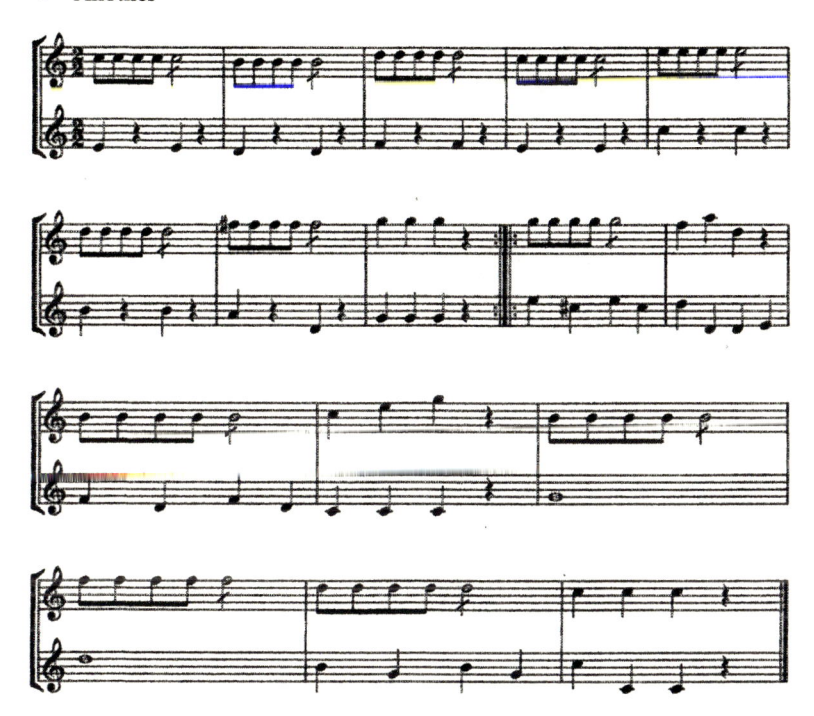

- Another

- Another

- Another

- Another

- Another

Observation

I believe I am obliged to place here the two following lessons, which are the most difficult to execute of all in this group. There is, however, a certain facility with regard to the movement that is restored to each group of two measures by four quarter notes. We will find likewise then all of the variations that the notes can make by their value in a measure of four beats. I encourage beginners to work often on following these two lessons, which will contribute greatly to their abilities to execute other pieces.[145]

---

[145] I have translated *l'engage* as "encourage"; its literal translation is "engage."

Moderato

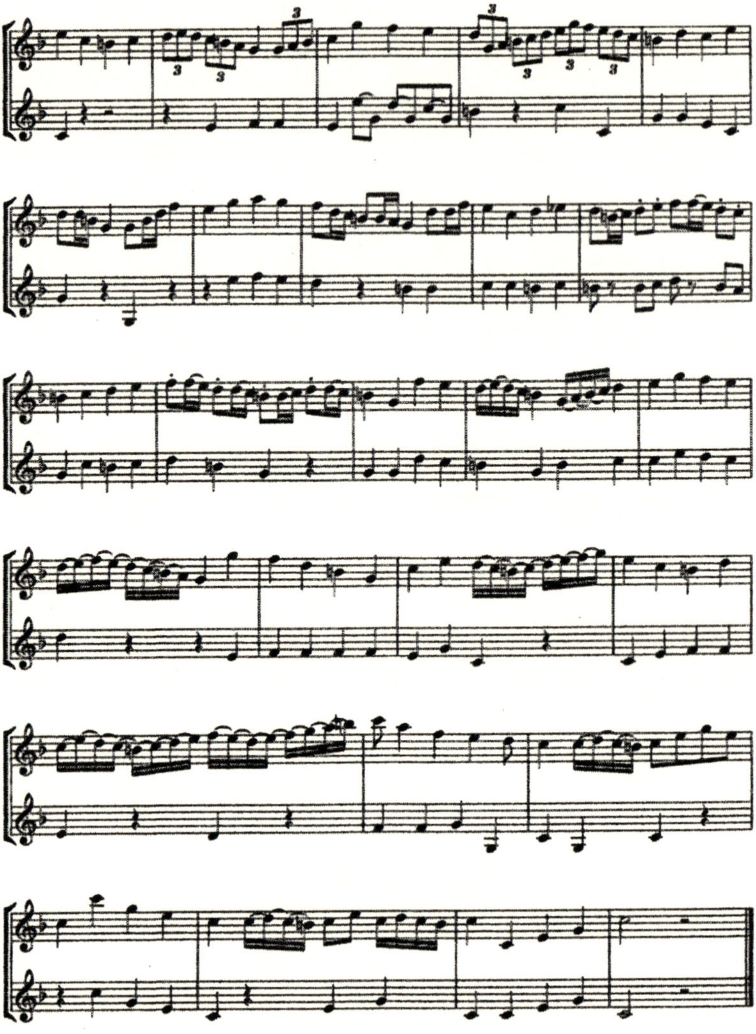
3
3
3
3
3
3
3

- Same genre; *Moderato*

Table of Comparison

The comparison of musical circumstances is most necessary for students and for understanding what I mean by the word "comparison." We must carefully examine the measures in the following table where we will see that No. 1 is similar to No. 2 by its execution although the notes are different as some are ascending while others are descending. It is thus their equal value in both measures that requires the same execution and which forms the comparison.

Because, for example, there is a difference in execution of the two following measures, this [musical notation] to that [musical notation], there will be equality in all of the measures that have the same rapport. There will no longer be any of the principles upon which the music would be rendered nearly incomprehensible. Here then is what proves that it is necessary to submit ourselves to the principles, for without them we have no execution at all.

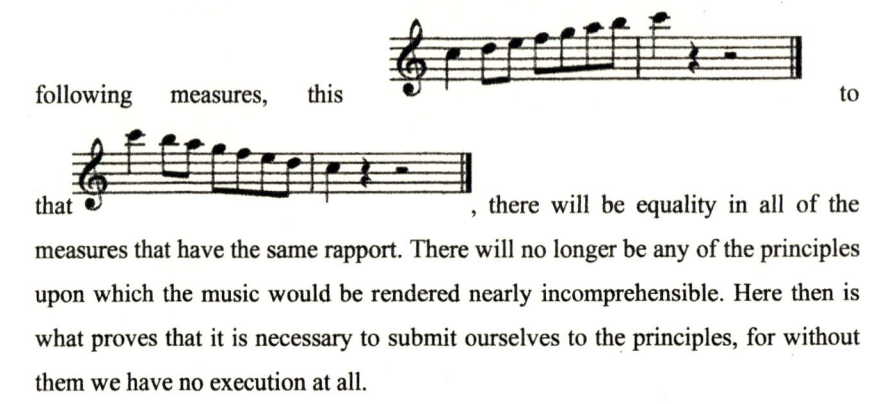

- Example

Relationship of the Clarinet to the Violin

This article is good to know in the case where we are obliged to transpose. For example, the clarinet in C does not transpose at all for its tone forms a unison with the violin, but it not the same for other longer or shorter clarinets. These last ones play several tones lower than the violin, and the longer clarinets, like in B♭ or in A, play several tones higher. Here is the table below.

- Clarinet in C: Scales in C, A minor, F, and D minor

203

- Clarinet in B♭: Scales in B♭, G minor, E♭, and C minor

[Musical notation: Violin and Clarinet, Scale in Bb]

[Musical notation: Violin and Clarinet, Scale in G minor]

[Musical notation: Violin and Clarinet, Scale in Eb]

[Musical notation: Violin and Clarinet, Scale in C minor]

Remarks:[146] This clarinet is much longer than the C clarinet. It is in B♭ and is lower in the bass by a tone. We are thus obliged consequently to play a whole tone higher in order to be in unison with the violin.

---

[146] B♭ clarinets are shorter in length than an A clarinet.

- Clarinet in A: Scales in A, F♯ minor, D, and B minor

It has a joint[147] in A, which is inserted onto the clarinet in B♭.

Remarks: This clarinet is longer than those in B♭ and is lower in the bass by two tones. It is necessary then to play two tones (a minor third) higher in order to be in unison with the violin.

---

[147] I have translated *corp* as "joint"; its literal translation is "body." It refers to the practice of using *corps de rechange*, interchangeable clarinet joints, to change the key of an instrument.

205

- Clarinet in B♮: Scales in E major, B major, G♯ minor, and C♯ minor

[Musical notation: Violin and Clarinet scales — Scale in E minor, Scale in B major, Scale in G♯ minor, Scale in C♯ minor]

It has a joint in B, which is played on the C clarinet.

Observation

We might need, for lack of a joint in B major, to use the A clarinet for playing in B major by playing two semitones higher. This is said to play in G major.

Remarks on the Clarinet in B Major

This clarinet is a half tone lower than the C clarinet or a tone lower than the violin. It is necessary as a result to play or write a half tone higher than the violin. Here it follows, as F natural makes for the clarinet a unison with the E natural of the violin, for by these means we avoid all of the sharps, which will be too difficult to produce on the clarinet.

There are still other clarinets, for example in G (clarinet d'amour or alto clarinet), but these are only instruments of fancy, which we do not use in orchestras. The clarinet in G is never used [for orchestral music]. The clarinets in E-flat and in F are employed only in military bands. Here meanwhile is the manner of writing these different instruments.

- Clarinet in G

This clarinet is very long and is lower in the bass register by a fourth (a major third).

- Clarinet in E♭: Scales for clarinet in B♭ and in E♭

This instrument is very short; it has the same manner of writing as for the horn

- Little Clarinet in F: The violin scale can also be played on C clarinet

The same manner of writing as for the horn

- Clarinet in D

Preludes

Preludes ordinarily announce the key in which the piece will be played, and ordinarily we begin a prelude by the tonic note that is made longer or shorter according to its capacity as you see below. Preludes are in the keys of C major, F major, D minor, C major, A minor, and G major.

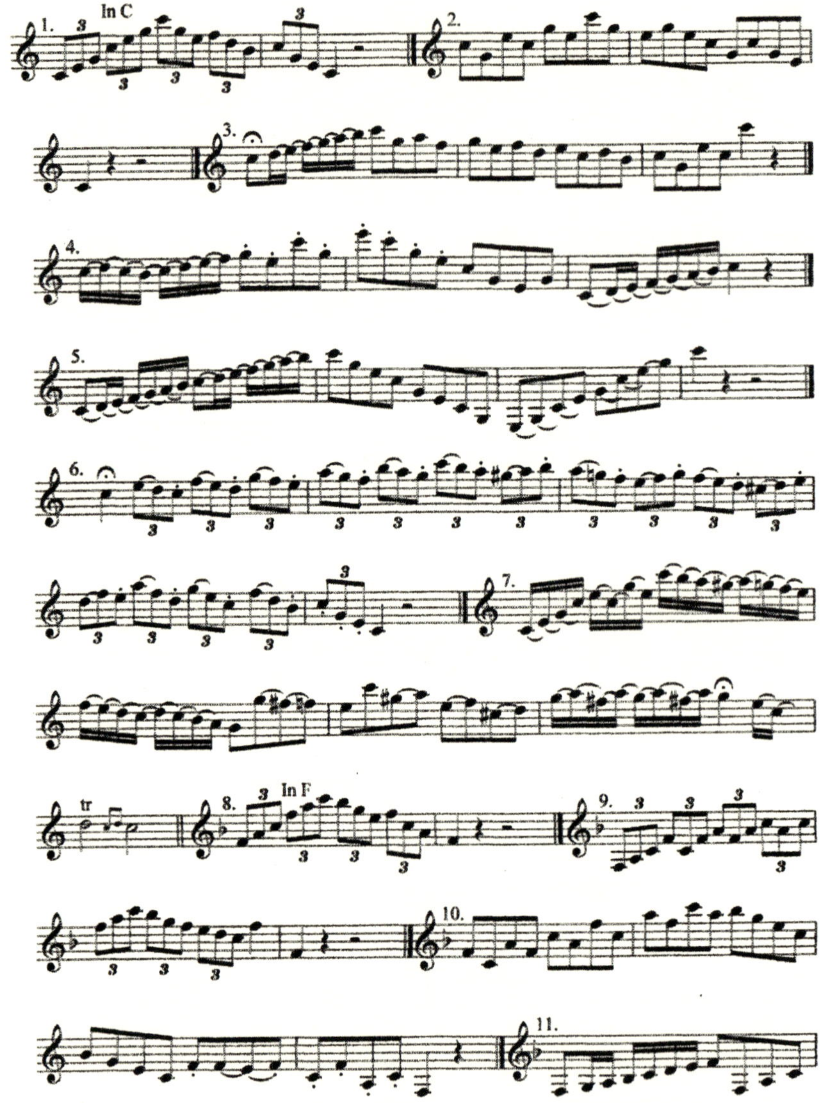
1.
In C
2.
3.
4.
5.
6.
7.
tr
8.
In F
9.
10.
11.

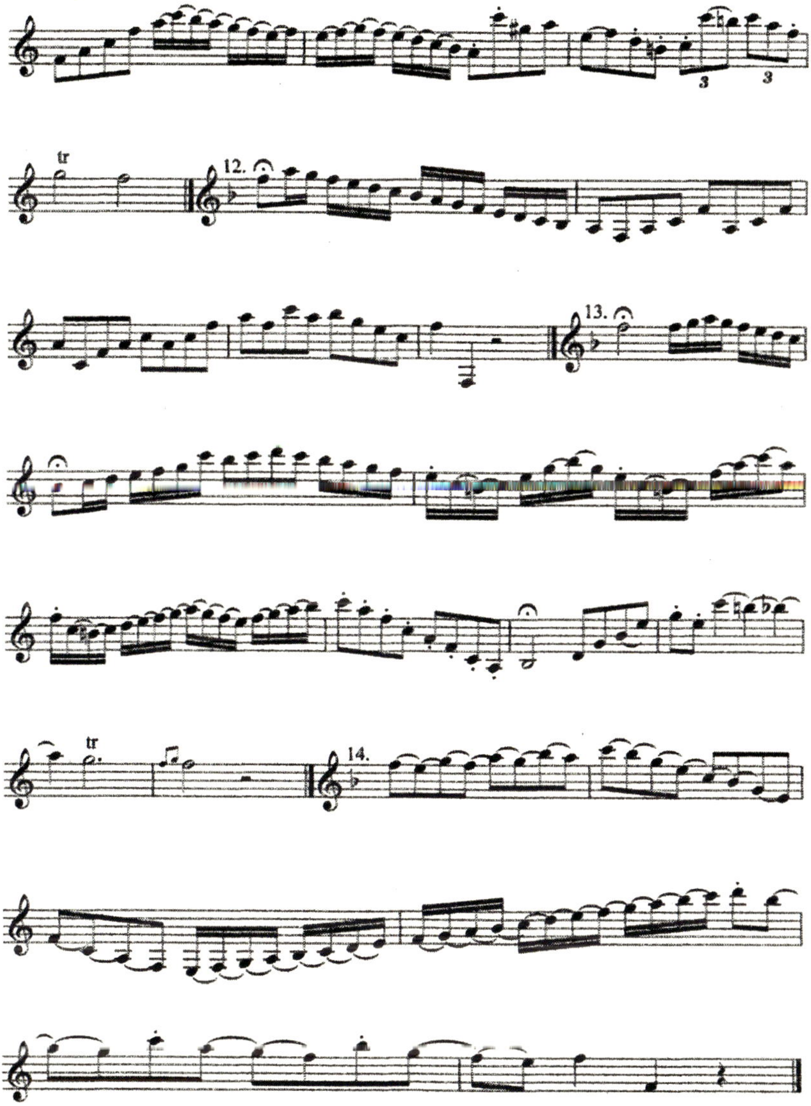
3
3
tr
12.
13.
tr
14.

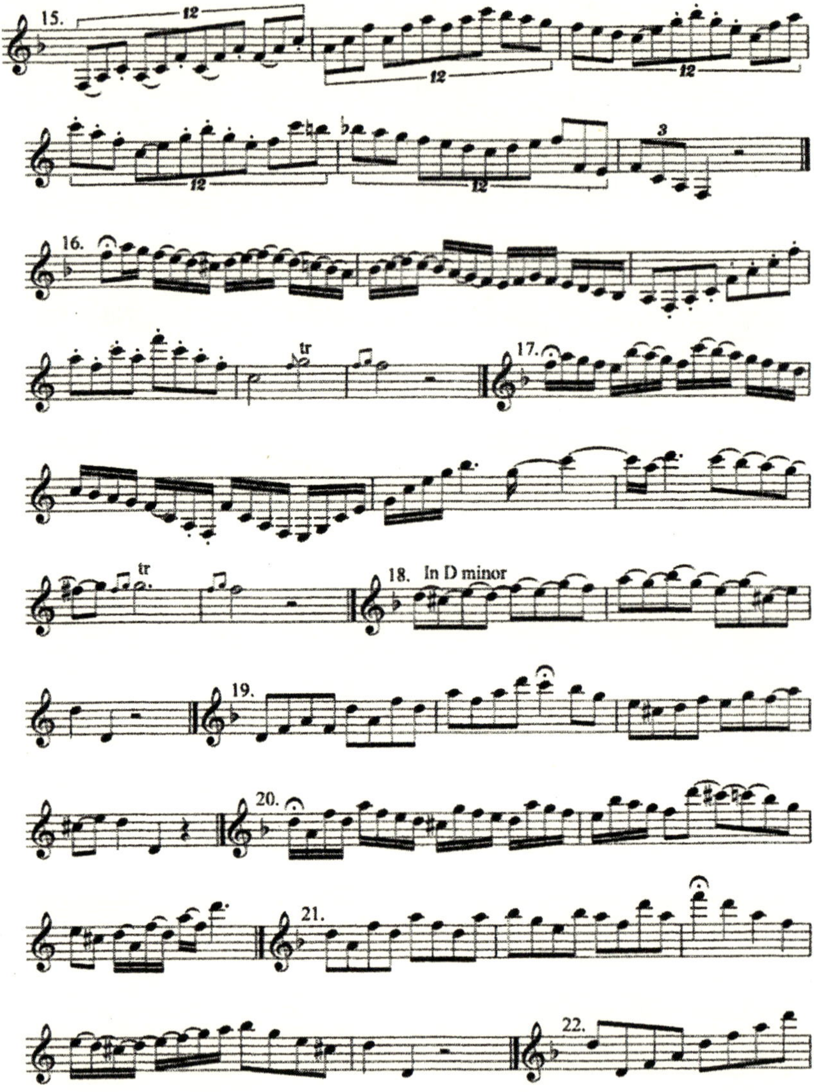
15.
12
3
16.
tr
17.
18. In D minor
19.
20.
21.
22.

211

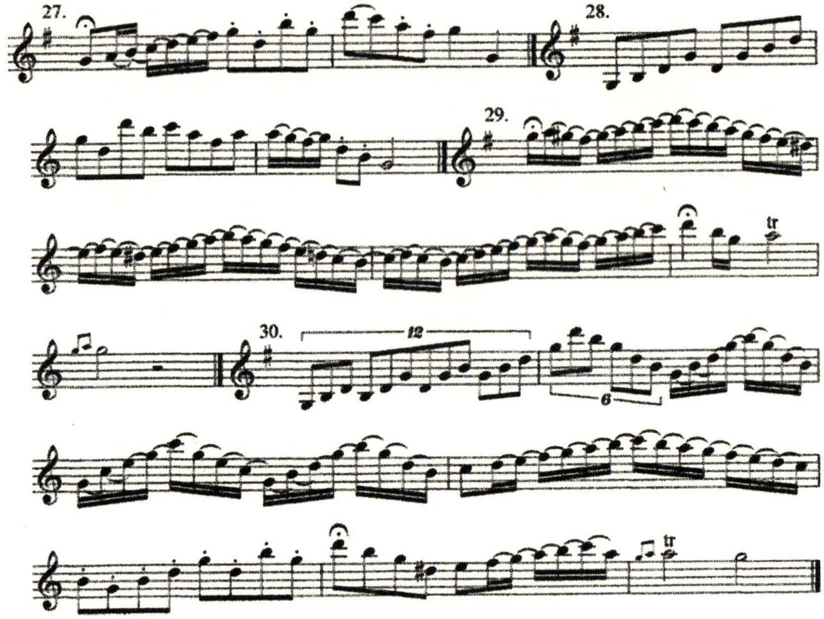
27.
28.
29.
tr
30.
12
6
tr

Chapter 4
A Commentary on *Méthode nouvelle et raisonnée pour la clarinette* and *Nouvelle méthode de clarinette*

Méthode nouvelle et raisonnée pour la clarinette (1785)

Vanderhagen's introduction to *Méthode nouvelle et raisonnée pour la clarinette* provides a brief description of contents including reeds, embouchure, tone quality, and articulation. Such specific introductory information emphasizes both the novelty of having a treatise solely written for the clarinet and the author's importance as a clarinet pedagogue. Vanderhagen also mentions that musical exercises in the form of short etudes and duos, helpful to the advanced student, can be found at the end of the work. He signs his title page "Amand Vanderhagen, Musician in the French Ordinary Guard of the King,"[148] indicating his status as an important performer and trustworthy teacher because of his high-ranking musical position.

This treatise consists of twelve chapters of varying lengths:

First Article: *Positioning the Arms and Head*
Second Article: *On the Embouchure*
Third Article: *The Quality of Reeds for Beginners*
Fourth Article: *Manner of Acquiring a Good Sound*
Fifth Article: *Different Articulations*
Sixth Article: *Triplets or Three-in-One*
Seventh Article: *Appoggiaturas*
Eighth Article: *The Accent*
Ninth Article: *Grace Notes*
Tenth Article: *[Reeds]*
Eleventh Article: *The Trill*
Twelfth Article: *Mordents*

---

[148] "Amand Van-Der-Hagen, Musicien de la Garde françoise Ordinaire du Roy." Vanderhagen, *Méthode nouvelle*, title page.

214

Although Vanderhagen provides instructions and musical examples for teaching concepts like meter, articulation, and transposition, he does not include the basic fundamentals of music, such as clefs, names of notes, and instructions for reading different clefs. A chart, placed immediately after the title page, provides fingerings, but no additional information is given on this subject. The lack of instruction on how to read music implies that Vanderhagen was writing for students who already possessed a basic knowledge of the fundamentals.

In the first article, Vanderhagen discusses proper body position for playing the clarinet. He emphasizes the importance of this subject by including the phrase "and most essential"[149] in the article's title. Students are urged to keep their bodies in a natural and relaxed position and to bring the clarinet up to their mouth rather than contorting their bodies. Vanderhagen explains that holding the clarinet in this manner keeps the hands and wrists flexible to allow for efficient movement between notes. Students are also reminded to keep their fingers close to the holes at all times to maintain proper hand position, which prevents sloppy technique. These concepts are virtually identical to those used in modern pedagogy,[150] as players are taught to "bring the clarinet to you, not yourself to the clarinet." A strong emphasis is also placed today on developing correct hand position to minimize unnecessary movement and prevent physical injury.

On the Embouchure, Vanderhagen's second article, concerns the practice of playing the clarinet with the reed against the top lip. He warns that the mouthpiece should be placed into the mouth only up to the shoulder of the reed (the line of division between the shaved cane and the bark) because an excess of mouthpiece in the mouth will cause the student to control the reed through biting

---

[149] "...et très essentiel." Ibid., 2.

[150] There are numerous method and pedagogy books available today that echo Vanderhagen's teachings. Some of the more notable books include Thomas Ridenour, *The Educator's Guide to the Clarinet*, (Denton, TX: T. Ridenour, 2000); David Pino, *The Clarinet and Clarinet Playing*, (New York: C. Scribner's Sons, 1980); Larry Guy, *The Daniel Bonade Workbook*, (Stony Point, NY: Rivernote Press, 2004), and Frederick John Thurston, *Clarinet Technique*, (London: Oxford University Press, 1964).

rather than using lip pressure. Vanderhagen instructs that the top teeth should rest on the reed to aid in playing high notes and that the sides of the embouchure should remain just firm enough to prevent air leakage. Contemporary practice also discourages air leakage from the embouchure, while lip pressure remains vital to the production and timbre of sound. Vanderhagen's comment about using the teeth to produce high notes is another technique used in modern clarinet performance today. Although the use of this technique is infrequent, there are occasions where direct teeth-to-reed pressure must be used in order to reach pitches well outside of the clarinet's normal range.

The third article presents a brief, yet informative, overview on reeds. Vanderhagen advises the student to select reeds that are soft enough to be played on comfortably without "sounding like a duck."[151] His advice to find a reed that plays well in the first octave of the clarinet may reflect a more newly prominent use of this particular range of the instrument at this time. Music for what is now deemed "the Baroque clarinet" typically covered a range of only about a tenth because of the instrument's physical limitations and loss of sound quality. By Vanderhagen's time, the clarinet had undergone major advancements in range and tonal quality, with most music written for it during this period reflecting these enhancements. Vanderhagen's advice on choosing this type of a reed may also stem from the fact that beginners spend most of their time playing within the first octave and would need a reed that will be responsive and free blowing. This advice remains pertinent to current clarinet students, as is the claim that the high F, G, and A cannot be reached until the embouchure has been developed. Vanderhagen's comment that high notes above F are seldom encountered reflects the writing of composers since these notes are not especially difficult to produce on a five-keyed clarinet.

The fourth article, *Manner of Acquiring a Good Sound*, begins with Vanderhagen's amusing observation that playing the clarinet with a good sound

---

[151] "...car le son deviendroit trop canard." Ibid., 2.

will never be as painful to the listener as playing with a poor sound, regardless of the player's technical ability. He advises the student to avoid "rolling their fingers" (to move their fingers too quickly) and to begin by playing slowly with solid air support. The concept of swelling on each note reflects a common performance practice of the time, *messa di voce*, as well as mirrors the modern concept of long tones where a note or notes are isolated and played with extreme crescendos and decrescendos in order to solidify tone, embouchure control, and air support. His final comment about playing at a comfortable dynamic level creates a translational difficulty because of the phrase *à demi jeu*. Although its literal translation is "to half-play," suggesting a sub-tone, it actually refers to playing at a *mezzo-forte*, a dynamic level preferred to this day for long tones and exercises to build embouchure and air control without putting excessive strain on the player.

Vanderhagen's fifth article offers a succinct explanation of clarinet articulation: "Articulations are to wind instruments what the bow stroke is to string instruments."[152] His instruction to vocalize an articulation through the syllable "D" provides the student with a tangible sound concept, and he illustrates each articulation variation with a musical example. For rapid passages, Vanderhagen writes that the player may need to use "chest articulation," an eighteenth-century practice that articulated notes without the use of the tongue. He concludes by claiming that students should be prepared to vary their articulation patterns depending on their musical situation, a statement that illustrates Classical clarinet performance practice. This advice is also very practical, as students both then and now must learn how to manipulate articulation patterns as necessary when faced with difficult passages or tempos, or embouchure fatigue, as well as to add intensity and color to the music.

---

[152] "Le Coup de Langue est à l'Instrument a vent ce qu'est le coup d'archet aux Instrument a Cordes." Ibid., 4.

Vanderhagen turns to the subject of triple meter in his sixth article. Here he distinguishes slurs from legato and staccato articulation by mentioning how "D" produces long, connected notes while "T" creates short notes. Modern pedagogy also teaches these articulations through syllables like "D" and "T" because each syllable requires a different stroke of the tongue against the reed, thus affecting the length of the reed's vibrations and the resulting tone. Several musical examples are offered to demonstrate different articulation combinations for a variety of styles and tempos.

The seventh and eighth articles, *Appoggiaturas* and *The Accent*, are brief discussions of ornamentation that rely on musical examples to explain these concepts. Embellishment in the form of grace notes is the subject of the ninth article. Literally translated as "tasteful notes,"[153] grace notes are described in a fashion similar to extended tones and accents. Vanderhagen requests that grace notes be reserved for solo performance only, because the embellishment of ensemble music will create confusion and be aesthetically displeasing. Ornamentation was commonplace in eighteenth-century performance practice, as the reputation of a performer was often determined by their virtuosic embellishment.

The untitled tenth article disrupts the organization of the treatise by returning to the topic of reeds, a subject first encountered in the third article. Vanderhagen's advice on choosing reeds dispels any notion that early clarinetists were not concerned with reed quality. He writes that reeds should be evenly grained and spongy to allow for consistent moisture retention and sound vibration, and warns the player not to overpower the reed with the lip or to use ill-fitting reeds. Despite radical differences between late eighteenth-century and modern reeds, such advice is pertinent to many different reed styles.

Vanderhagen returns to the topic of embellishment in his final two articles on trills and mordents. The eleventh article's instruction that the trill should begin

---

[153] "Des Notes de Gout." Ibid., 10.

on the note above the trill note, start slowly, and move quickly towards its end reflects Classical performance practice as reflected in contemporary didactic works by François Devienne and Michel Corrette.[154] Trills on main notes during ascending passages are permitted, but Vanderhagen prefers upper-note trills for descending and cadential notes. Prepared trills are distinguished from main note trills in this article as being prepared by "lingering on the borrowed note" rather than being "attacked all at once."[155] Vanderhagen also offers an alternative fingering for trilling on A^4. The twelfth article, *Mordents*, is very brief and describes the ornament as being the "opposite of the trill on the subject of the borrowed note." As with articles seven, eight, and nine, musical examples comprise most of Vanderhagen's instruction on the subject.

A short discussion on scales in various time signatures, lessons on the equality of different note values, and transposition follows the final numbered article. Vanderhagen places the most emphasis on time signatures and the determining of which beats are strong or weak. The following section entitled *Lessons* continues this discussion by demonstrating how to divide duple and triple meters into smaller note values. Numerous musical examples are used to demonstrate divisions of the beat along with additional examples illustrating how to count dotted notes and rests. He reminds the student that, while all of the musical examples can be played at various tempos, they must be learned at *Adagio* to ensure accuracy. The relative lack of explanation, combined with the number of musical examples, seems to suggest that Vanderhagen envisioned the student discussing these concepts with a teacher. For a student with no prior musical training, such a "hands-on approach" could be problematic without additional assistance from another musician or instructor.

---

[154] François Devienne, *Nouvelle méthode théorique et pratique pour la flûte* (Paris, 1794); Michel Corrette, *Nouvelle édition, revüe corrigée et augmentée de la gamme de hautbois et de la clarinette* (Paris, 1773).

[155] "Préparer une Cadence, c'est avant que de batter, rester un peu de temp sur la note d'emprunt." Ibid., 12.

The treatise concludes with a discussion on transposition between differently pitched clarinets and the violin. Vanderhagen describes this section as "necessary for those who want to play parts of symphonies or accompany in concerts,"[156] and provides brief comments on which clarinets should be used for certain types of music. Vanderhagen also remarks that the clarinetist must be able to play flute and oboe parts, and that they must learn how to transpose correctly so that they will not be embarrassed.

The remainder of *Méthode nouvelle et raisonnée pour la clarinette* contains twelve brief and five lengthy duos that are composed for an advanced player. Vanderhagen's twelve short examples are arrangements of popular melodies from operas of that time. Three etudes are based on *Blaise et Babet, ou La suite des trois fermiers*, a *comédie français* that was performed throughout Europe and was an audience favorite at the *Opéra-Comique* in Paris until about 1827.[157] Vanderhagen remarks on *Romance de Blaise et Babet*, "C'est pour toi que je les arange."[158] *De Blaise et Babet* is taken from the aria "Lise chantoit dans la Prairie"[159] while the third melody, also entitled *De Blaise et Babet*, is an arrangement of Blaise's and Babet's duo "Chantons l'Hymen."[160] Vanderhagen uses the aria "*De la Rose fraiche et vermeille*" from another popular *opéra-comique, De L'Embaras des Richesses*, for his second melodic etude/duo.[161] These four etudes represent both Vanderhagen's skill as an arranger and his

---

[156] "Chose nescessaire pour ceux qui veulent jouer les Parties de Simphonies ou d'Accompagnement dans les Concerts." Ibid., 18.

[157] Nicolas Dezède, *Blaise et Babet, ou La suite des trois fermiers*, libretto by Jacques Marie Boutet de Monvel (Paris: Houbault, 1783).

[158] "It is for you that I have arranged this," Vanderhagen, 19.

[159] "Singing songs in the meadow," Ibid., 21.

[160] "Singing a hymn," Ibid., 22.

[161] A. E. M. Grétry, *L'Embaras des Richesses*, libretto by Lourdet de Santerre (Paris: P. de Lormel, 1782).

acknowledgement of public tastes for music that did not always favor the clarinet. Although Grétry includes clarinets in his score for *L'Embaras des Richesses*, Dezède does not list clarinets in any version of his published score for *Blaise et Babet*.

Three other duos appear to have been arranged from *Les Amours D'Été*, a divertissement from a *comédie italienne* published in 1781.[162] *Des Amours D'Été* is clearly presented twice, the first time with the aria "Que le jour est loin encore"[163] and the second with "Reste encore un moment."[164] The final duo, *Légèrement*, seems to be another melody from *Les Amours D'Été* because it follows the eleventh duo, *Des Amours D'Été*.

De Renaud Marche des Circassienes is an arrangement of *The March of the Amazons and Circassiens* from Antonio Sacchini's *Renaud*.[165] As seen before with Dezède, Sacchini does not use clarinets in his published score. *Du Corsaire*, subtitled "Que de maux loin de toi,"[166] is based on the first aria of *Le Corsaire* by Dalayrac.[167] The origins of *Des Deux Jumeaux* is uncertain, as the only known opera that has a similar title and was composed between 1780–85 is *Les Deux Jumeaux de Bergamo* by M. A. Desaugiers.[168] *Andantino*, the duo, which immediately follows *Des Deux Jumeaux*, seems to be another melody from this same opera. *Malbrouk*, the tenth duo, does not contain a subtitle and it is unclear from where this material was taken. This duo's melody has a similar melodic

---

[162] *Les Amours D'Été*, libretto by Piis U. Barré (Paris: Vente, 1781).

[163] "Where the day is more distant," Vanderhagen, 20.

[164] "Resting for a moment," Ibid., 22.

[165] Antonio Sacchini, *Renaud*, libretto by Jean Joseph Leboeuf (Paris: Théodore Michaelis, 1783; reprint, New York: Broude Brothers Limited, 1971).

[166] "Who is distant from you," Vanderhagen, 22.

[167] Nicolas Dalayrac, *Le Corsaire*, libretto by Chabeaussiére (Paris: Leduc, 1783).

[168] M. A. Desaugiers, *Les Deux Jumeaux de Bergamo*, libretto by Florian (Paris: n.p., 1782).

contour to a popular chanson of that era, *Malbrouk dans une Bouteille*, but given the close similarities between Vanderhagen's other arrangements and their original sources, this duo on *Malbrouk* does not appear to have been taken from the chanson version.[169] It seems probable that these duos represent some of Vanderhagen's previously published arrangements in his two-volume collection of operatic melodies for clarinet, *Receuils d'ariettes choisies* (1783).[170]

The final five duos are substantially longer than the twelve initial ones and do not appear to have any connection to operatic or popular melodies. These duos are not progressive in nature and are suited only for an advanced student. All of the duos use either 4/4 or 2/4 time with the exception of the fifth duo's *Andante*, which is in 3/4, and the only embellishments written into the parts are grace notes. Although Vanderhagen composes elegant, fluid melodies for his duos, his exercises are not embellished and require students to create their own ornaments.

Vanderhagen includes a postscript at the end of his treatise suggesting that once the student has completed his instruction manual he will become a better clarinetist than Vanderhagen. The student is then advised to turn to the music of Michel Yost, a fellow guard member and popular Parisian virtuoso, because his duos will teach "you everything that is possible to do on the clarinet."[171] This parting comment suggests that Vanderhagen was humble about his abilities and wished to publicly recognize Yost as a superior musician. It may also reflect a thinly veiled attempt by Vanderhagen to curry favor with his older, more prominent colleague.

---

[169] *Malbrouk dans une Bouteille (Parodie populaire)* in *La France Qui Chante: Airs et Paroles Recueillis Ou Choisis*, arr. H. E. Moore and H. Rodney Bennett (Boston: D. C. Heath and Company, 1924).

[170] Weston, *More Clarinet Virtuosi of the Past*, 262.

[171] "…ainsi que les Duo de M. Michel dans les quells on trouvera tout ce qu'il est possible de faire sur la Clarinette." Vanderhagen, *Méthode nouvelle*, 36.

Nouvelle méthode de clarinette (1799)

Vanderhagen's second treatise on the clarinet, *Nouvelle méthode de clarinette*, is considerably more substantial than his first. Comprised of two parts, the first focuses on how to play the clarinet and the second contains etudes and duos for an advanced student. Vanderhagen describes his second treatise as "containing all principles concerning this instrument as well as the principles of music, detailed with precision and clarity."[172] He includes a small personal introduction claiming that he wrote this treatise both because of his first treatise's popularity and out of the need to provide even better instruction on the clarinet. In the introduction Vanderhagen places emphasis on teaching fundamental concepts in music, indicating that he was now addressing an audience of beginners. These introductory remarks also reflect changing perceptions of the clarinet from a novelty instrument in 1785 that was learned after another instrument, such as flute, to a respected solo instrument by 1799 that could be studied by itself.

Nouvelle méthode has a different form than *Méthode nouvelle et raisonnée* in that the reader must progress through several paragraphs of information before reaching Article One. Despite a reordering of sections, most of Vanderhagen's information in this second treatise can be traced to his first. The overall form of the second treatise contains the following articles:

> First Article: *Concerning All the Signs of Which Music is Composed*
> Second Article: *Of the Value and the Shape of Notes*
> Third Article: [*Dotted Notes and Rests*]
> Fourth Article: [*Sharps and Flats*]
> Fifth Article: *Sequence of the Signs*
> Sixth Article: *On the Number of Sharps Which Are Necessary in Each Key, and to Relative Keys*
> Seventh Article: *On the Scale*
> Eighth Article: *What the Intervals are Composed of*

---

[172] "Contenant tous les principes concernant cet Instrument ainsi que les principes de la Musique, détaillés avec précision et clarté." Vanderhagen, *Nouvelle méthode*, title page.

> Ninth Article: *Instruction on What All of the Inverted Intervals of Minor and Major, and the Augmented and Diminished Intervals, Become*
> Tenth Article: *Definitions of Italian Terms That Are Used for Indicating Movements and Nuances*
> Eleventh Article: *The Measure*
> Twelfth Article: *On Breathing*
> Thirteenth Article: *Of Articulations and of the Slur*
> Fourteenth Article: *Of Appoggiaturas and Other Grace Notes*
> Fifteenth Article: *The Trill and the Turn*
> Sixteenth Article: *Lessons on Rests*
> Seventeenth Article: *On Syncopation*

Vanderhagen also includes several paragraphs prior to his first article, which include.

> *Observation of the Author on this Second Publication*
> *Natural Scale-Explanation of the Scale*
> *Scale on the Sharps and Flats*
> *Advice for Beginners*
> *On the Position of the Body, the Arms, and the Head–A Preliminary Observation*
> *Embouchure*
> *The First Lesson on the Instrument–An Observation*
> *Principles of Music on the Knowledge of Notes*
> *Different Scales*
> *Connected Steps*

Vanderhagen begins his second treatise with an explanation of how to read his fingering chart. He also sensibly points out a useful trill fingering in the text since it is not included in either of his fingering charts. His comments are quite helpful to beginning and moderately advanced clarinetists.

Advice for Beginners begins with a timeless caveat to students about how they must be patient and diligent in learning how to play the clarinet. Vanderhagen's comment, "do not torment him to let you play songs from opera or other popular melodies much too soon,"[173] probably reflects his frustration over trying to teach impatient and unskilled students.

Vanderhagen's *On the Position of the Body, the Arms, and the Head–A Preliminary Observation* offers the same approach to teaching a beginning student that modern instructors use. Teaching the student to first form an embouchure and then hold the instrument allows them to immediately begin grasping fundamental concepts of clarinet playing. Vanderhagen's advice that once students have become fatigued they should alternate between learning music and the clarinet also remains a teaching technique used today. The descriptions of proper body posture are essentially the same as those found in the first treatise, with a brief mention here of how the fingers must remain close to the keys and tone holes because some notes must be produced through the embouchure (i.e., some notes are produced through biting and over-blowing).

Vanderhagen's opening remarks concerning the importance of the embouchure are remarkably forward thinking, considering that modern pedagogy focuses on the same concepts:

> The clarinet is not a difficult instrument up to a certain point, but it is also not one of the easiest when we want to attain a certain degree of perfection. That is impossible to obtain if we do not have a good embouchure that is synonymous with a good sound. It is for this that the student must work from the beginning, for the embouchure is the basis of all wind instruments.[174]

---

[173] "Ne le tourmentés pas pour qu'il vois fasse jouer trop tôt des airs d'opera, ou autres airs connus, car je connoit par une assez longue experience, le foible des commençants à ce sujet." Ibid., 4.

[174] "La Clarinette n'est pas un instrument bien difficile jusqu'a certain point, mais il n'est pas non plus des plus aisés, quant on veut atteindre un certain degré de perfection qui est impossible d'obtenir si l'on n'a pas une belle embouchure ce qui est sinonime avec un beau son. C'est donc à cela qu'il faut travailler des le commencement, car l'embouchure est la bâse de tous les instruments à vent." Ibid., 6.

His closing section on choosing appropriate reeds, as in the earlier treatise, also enjoys a direct connection to current methods of teaching, as does his comment that "you must search for a good compromise by taking a very strong reed and weakening it by shaving it a little with a penknife."[175]

In *The First Lesson on the Instrument: An Observation*, Vanderhagen offers a remarkable concept by stating that students should begin on the bass notes of the instrument: "It will always be preferable, in my opinion, to begin in the bass, because the two thumbs, as well as the fingers, are employed which gives a certain aplomb for holding the instrument."[176] Most instructional methods on the clarinet today have the student begin by playing G^4, also known as "open G," because this pitch can be produced with little effort. However, as this note does not involve any fingers, it creates problems for the student because they do not have a secure grip on the instrument with their hands, nor are they comfortable yet with their embouchure. Vanderhagen's recommendation that a student begin with "the bass notes" solves these problems by allowing the student to firmly grasp the clarinet with both hands. Starting with low notes also helps teach air support and embouchure because these pitches are not as easy to produce as G. Despite the publication date of 1799, this section displays a stronger and more effective teaching approach than most contemporary clarinet methods that begin a student on "open G."

The intended audience of this second treatise becomes apparent in *Principles of Music on the Knowledge of Notes*, as Vanderhagen's explanation of treble, bass, and alto clefs are part of his general introduction to music fundamentals. He remarks that students should learn to play various pitches in random orders to solidify their memory of note names and fingerings. The

---

[175] "Il faut donc chercher un juste milieu prendre un canche plus forte que foible parce qu'il est trés facile de la mettre au point convenable en la gratant un peu avec un canif." Ibid., 7.

[176] "Mais Il vaut toujours mieux selon moi, de commencer par le bas, par la raison que les deux mais sont employez, ainsi que les doigts et que cela donne un certain aplomb pour tenir l'instrument." Ibid., 7.

following section, on *Different Scales*, encourages the student to practice both conjunct and disjunct scales.

The first article, *Concerning All the Signs of Which Music is Composed*, continues Vanderhagen's preliminary instruction on music fundamentals by discussing clefs, note values and names, and meter. His explanation of G, B, and C clefs reflects the practice of shifting a clef sign to keep more notes within the staff, but he does not mention any relationship between clarinets in different keys and the G, B, and C clefs.

The second and third articles use pyramid-shaped charts to show the divisions of notes and rests. These charts provide a clear and easily understandable pictorial explanation of how notes and rests are subdivided into smaller units.

A lengthy discussion on sharps and flats occurs in the fourth article including information on how they function, their arrangement in the circle of fourths or fifths, and their ability to be doubled. The concept of determining a key signature through the presence of accidentals is also briefly mentioned, although Vanderhagen refers the reader to his sixth article for more information on this topic. The section concludes with his claim that sharps, flats, and naturals are nothing more than accidental signs unless they are specified in the key signature.

Sequence of the Signs, the fifth article, gives a very brief explanation of musical signs including the repeat sign and *da capo*. Slurs, staccato, and the crescendo and decrescendo are also mentioned, although these signs are demonstrated mostly through musical examples.

Further explanation of accidentals and keys occurs in the sixth article, *On the Number of Sharps Which Are Necessary in Each Key, and to Relative Keys*. Vanderhagen's descriptions of how to calculate the mode and tonic note of a key are rather stilted because he writes lengthy run-on sentences without punctuation, although his accompanying musical examples help to clarify these concepts.

227

The seventh article, *On The Scale*, deals with the arrangement of whole and half steps in the scale. Vanderhagen also discusses how chords can be inverted and rearranged. The eighth article, *What the Intervals are Composed of*, provides numerous musical examples displaying different types of intervals.

Articles Nine and Ten, *Instruction on What All of the Inverted Intervals of Minor and Major, and the Augmented and Diminished Intervals, Become*, and *Definitions of Italian Terms that are Used for Indicating Movements and Nuances*, consist of lists of intervals and musical terms. Vanderhagen presents his paragraph on intervals in a Socratic dialogue, while his musical terms and phrases are arranged in a column without any apparent order.

In his eleventh article, Vanderhagen emphasizes the importance of "the measure:"

> The measure is so necessary in execution that by altering it too much we make even the best-known melody unrecognizable. Attaching all of your attention to this principle is essential, and be persuaded that to play poorly but in time is preferable to divine playing where no tempo is observed.[177]

He also maintains that a musical beat can be marked for vocalists by the hand, but that instrumentalists must tap out the beat using their toes. This concept of silent beating with the toe inside of a shoe is still taught by teachers seeking to avoid ungainly foot tapping among their students. Vanderhagen's statement that "only conductors are permitted an obvious beat"[178] certainly brings a sense of humor to this article since the problem of "instrumentalist conductors" remains an issue to this day.

---

[177] "La mesure est si nécessaire dans l'éxecution qu'en l'alterant par trop on rendroit m'éconnoissable l'Air même le plus connu; attaché toute votre attention à ce principe essensiel, et soyez persuadé qu'un jeu médiocre mais en mesure, est préferable à un jeu divin lors qu'on n'en observeroit aucune." Ibid., 22.

[178] "Il n'est permis qu'à celui qui conduit, de la batter distinctement." Ibid., 22.

The twelfth article begins by focusing on teaching the student how to find an appropriate place to breathe during a musical phrase. Vanderhagen advises that breaths should be taken between slurs or after cadences to maintain a smooth phrase. He finishes this section by claiming that breaths should be taken whenever the opportunity arises to prevent "emergency breaths" that break-up a phrase, create lung fatigue, and encourage improper breathing by gasping. A teacher today often refers to this concept as "breathing when necessary."

Several intermittent paragraphs are given between the twelfth and thirteenth articles on topics including disjunct degrees, chromatic notes, the bass and chalumeau notes of the clarinet, and the inverted perfect chord. In *Disjunct Degrees*, Vanderhagen discusses the differences and similarities in fingerings between registers. His comment that "E of the bass and the B on the third line use the same fingering" reflects the fact that the clarinet over-blows at the twelfth, rather than the octave as other wind instruments do. His lesson on chromatic notes presents musical examples, and the following *Observation* contains a mixture of examples on keys and meters with a reminder to beat time using the foot or toe. Vanderhagen briefly mentions the lower pitches of the clarinet as being "essential" in performance, and he concludes this section by presenting musical examples of a triad and its various inversions. Inverting the entire previous study creates some of these musical exercises. As in earlier sections, the presentation of these paragraphs seems to suggest that Vanderhagen intended for this material to be supplemented by a teacher's instruction.

The thirteenth article, *Of Articulations and of the Slur*, teaches how to express legato and staccato articulations through the syllables of "Tee" and "Tuh." This concept of learning articulations through vocalizing syllables parallels modern pedagogy, as do Vanderhagen's musical examples. The variety of articulation possibilities presented offers insight for clarinetists studying music from the high Classical period. It also illustrates possibilities for personal variation in performance, as well as offering potential "articulation solutions" to difficult passages.

The fourteenth article, which discusses grace notes and extended tones, serves as a shortened reprise of the first treatise's articles on these topics. Article Fifteen, *The Trill and the Turn*, also summarizes information taken from the first treatise, although here Vanderhagen also presents turns, along with a brief lesson on reading dotted notes (i.e., a dotted half note equals three quarter notes, etc.). Musical examples are presented throughout both articles to help illustrate these concepts and perhaps to compensate for the lack of written descriptions.

Lessons on Rests, the sixteenth article, begins with Vanderhagen's ageless observation that miscounted rests can ruin a performance while rests of short durations are difficult to count precisely. He also offers the sage advice that clarinetists must fit their parts into the overall texture by carefully following the accompaniment. Several counting exercises are then given, followed by an *Observation* and duos. Vanderhagen's comment that the student should alternate between the first and second parts of the duos allows the student to both practice reading different melodic lines and learn how to collaborate with another musician (e.g., their teacher). This type of student-teacher interaction remains an important element in contemporary pedagogy.

The seventeenth article relies mostly on its musical examples to demonstrate the concept of syncopation. Vanderhagen provides two lessons under *Observation* that further demonstrate syncopation and serve as student exercises for practicing this technique. He suggests that the note before the syncopation should be shortened in order to make the syncopation more expressive, a valuable comment that remains excellent advice to the modern musician. The following section, *Table of Comparison*, offers a series of musical examples that use notes from a C-major scale to display various rhythmic possibilities.

Vanderhagen's final section in this treatise, *Relationship of the Clarinet with the Violin*, discusses transpositions for clarinets pitched in C, B♭, A, B, G,

E♭, F, and D. The descriptions of these instruments document how clarinets were built and used during this time period. Vanderhagen specifically states that the A clarinet is created with a *corps de rechange* inserted into the B♭ clarinet and the B clarinet is created with a *corps de rechange* inserted into the C clarinet. The use of *corps de rechange* mirrors the use of crooks on natural horns to increase the flexibility of the instrument in various keys. This practice was gradually abandoned during the nineteenth century due to advances in instrument building such as additional keys and the invention of the Boehm system. The remainder of *Nouvelle méthode de clarinette* contains etudes and duos that are suitable only for an advanced student. Unlike the 1785 treatise these musical exercises do not appear to have been based on operatic or popular melodies.

Although *Nouvelle méthode de clarinette* contains more information on music fundamentals than *Méthode nouvelle et raisonnée pour la clarinette*, its articles on clarinet playing, including embouchure, body posture, and reeds, are essentially a reworking of those found in the first treatise. Much of Vanderhagen's advice and musical examples in both treatises is applicable to contemporary pedagogy. His writings are also remarkably forward thinking for their time, especially given that other French materials on the clarinet written before and during this time fail to address even the most basic elements of clarinet pedagogy. Although Vanderhagen's language and musical examples may first appear awkward by modern conventions, the only sections that contain truly archaic performance practices include the discussions of playing with the reed on the top of the mouthpiece and some cross- and alternate fingerings (found in the fingering charts and periodically in musical examples on trills and other embellishments).

Vanderhagen's treatises offer valuable insight into Classical clarinet playing, and, despite the presence of a few articles that are not applicable by current standards, contain a great deal of information that is relevant to modern pedagogy. *Méthode nouvelle et raisonnée pour la clarinette* and *Nouvelle méthode de clarinette* are remarkable sources that fully display Vanderhagen's importance as a performer and pedagogue for both Classical and modern clarinetists. They are also the first real methods to be written for the instrument, establishing a template for all future pedagogical writings.

Chapter 5
The Relationship Between the Treatises of Vanderhagen, Blasius, and Lefèvre

Although the extent to which Vanderhagen's methods affected clarinetists of the Classical era has yet to be determined, there is compelling evidence that his writings significantly influenced his immediate contemporaries. This impact can be documented in some cases by paraphrase or direct plagiarism of his writings and musical examples. Reproduction of printed material was a common occurrence at this time and, given the prominence of Vanderhagen's treatises, particularly his *Méthode nouvelle et raisonnée pour la clarinette* (1785), it is not surprising that other authors or publishers would have imitated or copied his work. The amount of material borrowed from his two clarinet treatises may also indicate the esteem with which his contemporaries regarded Vanderhagen. Two popular instructional treatises published within a few years of Vanderhagens', Frédéric Blasius's *Nouvelle méthode de clarinette et raisonnement des instruments* and Jean Xavier Lefèvre's *Méthode de clarinette*, reproduce his material to varying degrees.

Matthieu Frédéric Blasius (1758–1829) was a violinist, composer, and conductor who, like Vanderhagen, played clarinet in the *Garde Nationale*. He became a professor at the new *Conservatoire de Musique* from 1795–1802, and served as a conductor and director for the *Garde Consulaire* and *Garde Imperiale*.[178] Staffing cuts at the *Conservatoire* resulted in Blasius's dismissal in 1802. Published in 1796, *Nouvelle méthode de clarinette et raisonnement des instruments* is Blasius's only known instructional treatise and is dedicated to his

---
[178] Weston, 52–53.

students at the *Conservatoire de Musique*. Divided into twelve articles, the treatise uses a Socratic dialogue to teach basic concepts of music. William Menkin, in his analysis of this treatise, writes:

> Blasius's inspiration for publishing *Nouvelle méthode* was probably due to problems encountered in his teaching at the Conservatory. Judging from the attitude and scope of the method, Blasius was attempting to train marginally talented performers. The pedagogy is oriented towards gaining mere competency, and requires no previous background for understanding. Such things reflect the intellectual competence of his students as his need to write out in words where each finger was to be placed rather than trusting an understanding of the usual diagrams of the fingering chart.[179]

Jean Xavier Lefèvre (1763–1829) was also a clarinetist in the band of the *Garde Françoise du Roi* and the *Garde Nationale*. Well-known as a virtuoso, Léfèvre performed numerous concerts in Paris and composed a large number of concertos, duos, and trios for clarinet. He served as a professor of clarinet at the *Conservatoire de Musique* from 1795 to 1825, and is generally credited with being the most important French clarinet teacher of the nineteenth century.[180] *Méthode de clarinette*, his only instructional treatise, was published in 1802. Written for the six-keyed clarinet, his *Méthode* was accepted unanimously by a Conservatory committee, including Blasius, to be used as the school's only clarinet method.[181] Lefèvre's treatise was used throughout Europe until the 1930s and is still cited for pedagogical and research purposes because of the strength and clarity of his teachings.

---

[179] Menkin, 15–16.

[180] Weston, 160–61.

[181] Lowell Youngs, "Jean Xavier Lefèvre: His Contributions to the Clarinet and Clarinet Playing" (DMA thesis, The Catholic University of America, 1970), 32.

Structure

Blasius, although his *Nouvelle méthode de clarinette et raisonnement des instruments* contains twelve articles like Vanderhagen's *Méthode nouvelle et raisonnée pour la clarinette*, does not present the same information. Basic musical concepts like clef signs, note names, and note and rest values are slowly taught through a Socratic dialogue. Lefèvre's *Méthode de clarinette* does share similarities to Vanderhagen's organization, as seven of fourteen articles in his treatise discuss subjects identical to those of Vanderhagen. Information on body posture, forming an embouchure, selecting reeds, playing with a good sound, articulation, embellishments, phrasing, and breathing are presented in an order reminiscent of Vanderhagen's *Méthode nouvelle et raisonnée pour la clarinette*. Lefèvre's advice in these sections, although it echoes much of the information given by Vanderhagen, such as choosing a reed that is neither too hard nor too soft, does not seem to borrow from either of Vanderhagen's treatises. The similarity of presentation between these works suggests that Lefèvre was familiar with Vanderhagen's work and may have used the 1785 treatise as a template for his own.[182]

Fingering Charts

Vanderhagen offers two small fingering charts in his 1785 treatise, one of natural notes and a second of chromatic notes. A picture of a five-keyed clarinet accompanies each chart with its parts labeled. The 1799 treatise contains two almost identical charts to those of the 1785 work, although each chart is there much larger in size, and the chart of chromatic notes has been extended upwards from E-flat^6 to F-sharp^6. The clarinet shown next to each chart is still a five-keyed instrument, and for both charts alternative fingerings are discussed for D^6 in the chart of natural notes and C-sharp^6 in the chart of chromatic notes.

Blasius offers two fingering charts as well, each comprising a page, for natural notes and chromatic notes. These charts are extremely similar to the charts

---

[182] Please refer to Appendix Three for a complete listing of contents for all four treatises.

used in Vanderhagen's 1799 treatise through the alignment of notes on dotted lines and in the use of identical clarinet pictures. Blasius omits Vanderhagen's labeling of the clarinet's parts, however, and his chart for natural notes features below it an additional listing of three alternative fingerings for D^6, an element found only in the natural notes chart from Vanderhagen's 1785 treatise. The chart of natural notes also gives a brief discussion on these alternative fingerings for D^6. Overall similarities suggest that Blasius relied heavily on Vanderhagen's charts to create his own.[183]

Lefèvre owes a great deal to Vanderhagen's fingerings even though he was the first writer to provide a chromatic range from E to C^4 (considered the present-day standard range), and includes a chromatic trill chart to E^3. Two charts are given, one for natural notes and one for a complete chromatic scale, and each chart is printed on a long sheet of paper that could be folded out from the binding. The chart of natural notes has extended the range of the clarinet by two pitches, from A^6 to C^7, and four alternate fingerings for D^6 are offered. Lefèvre includes chromatic mordents between notes in his chart of chromatic notes, and in both charts dotted lines are drawn from the fingerings to the picture of the clarinet to indicate which fingers are used for each note.

Musical Examples

Several of Vanderhagen's musical examples, particularly those from his 1799 treatise, are reused in Blasius's treatise. One example occurs in Blasius's section on the value of notes, where he essentially copies Vanderhagen's Second Article, "Of the Value and the Shape of Notes." Although both the simple side-to-side comparison of note values by Vanderhagen and his "note pyramids" have been rewritten by Blasius into his Socratic dialogue, these changes are very slight. Other examples that are closely imitated include Blasius's section on intervals, taken from Vanderhagen's Eighth Article, "What the Intervals are Composed of,"

---

[183] Albert Rice offers a discussion of Vanderhagen's and Blasius's fingerings in "Clarinet Fingering Charts, 1732–1816," *Galpin Society Journal* 37 (1984), 26–26.

and Blasius's article on transposition, which reflects Vanderhagen's passage on the same subject. Lefèvre does not imitate any of Vanderhagen's musical examples, although some examples, such as those for trills, appear similar because they illustrate these concepts for specific notes. Musical studies, such as etudes and exercises, are not copied between Vanderhagen, Blasius, or Lefèvre, indicating that each author wrote their own practice studies based on their own pedagogical practices.

Concepts of Instruction

The process of identifying articles and concepts that could have been influenced by Vanderhagen's treatises can be difficult.[184] Passages of information between treatises often appear similar because they are addressing standard pedagogical issues. Blasius's fourth article, which discusses the effect of sharps and flats on a note, carries a strong resemblance to Vanderhagen's fourth article in his 1799 treatise, "Accidental Signs." The musical example on C^5 is used in both treatises, with the only difference occurring in Blasius's addition of the word "mineur." Vanderhagen illustrates C, C-flat, and C-natural as "The natural note–the same lowered a half pitch because of the flat–the same raised a half pitch and returned to its natural pitch because of the natural," while Blasius describes the same three notes as "The natural note–the same lowered a half pitch minor because of the flat–the same raised a half pitch and returned to its natural pitch because of the natural."[185] Another difference between these examples in the treatises occurs in the way Blasius uses C^5 rather than Vanderhagen's E^6 and

---

[184] Recommended studies on eighteenth-century pedagogy include: Betty Bang Mather and David Lasocki, *The Art of Preluding 1700–1830* (New York: McGinnis and Marx Music Publishers, 1984); Betty Bang Mather and David Lasocki, *Free Ornamentation in Woodwind Music 1700–1775* (New York: McGinnis and Marx Music Publishers, 1976); Betty Bang Mather, *Interpretation of French Music from 1675 to 1775* (New York: McGinnis and Marx Music Publishers, 1973); and Frederick Neumann, *Performance Practices of the Seventeenth and Eighteenth Centuries* (New York: Schirmer Books, 1993).

[185] "Note naturel, la même note baissée d'un demi ton mineur par le moyen du bemol, la même note baissée d'un demi ton ou mise dans son ton naturel par le moyen du Becare" (Blasius, *Nouvelle méthode de clarinette et raisonement des instruments* [1796], 15).

again by use of "mineur" in describing how a sharp or flat works. Other close similarities can be observed between Vanderhagen and Blasius's explanations on the intervals of a scale. Although the musical examples in each treatise are engraved in different formats (Vanderhagen shows intervals on a continuous line while Blasius presents each interval separately), the general presentation of these articles is complimentary to each other. Blasius seems to have copied Vanderhagen literally in his brief discussion on turns, as here he uses almost all of Vanderhagen's text and one of his musical examples. The article on the value of notes is also an example of Blasius's strong imitation of Vanderhagen's 1799 treatise, as discussed above.

Vanderhagen's 1785 treatise also resurfaces in Blasius's work in his articles on body posture and forming an embouchure. Although Blasius has condensed Vanderhagen's writing to create shorter paragraphs that combine his teachings on both subjects, the similarity of phrasing and wording suggests that Blasius relied on Vanderhagen for this information:

> It is necessary for the clarinet to have a reed that is not too hard, in order that one can conquer the tones that are found either too high or too low. Because, if you have a hard reed, you will spoil the lips and fatigue your chest without succeeding to pull one single sound from this instrument which is pleasurable. Whereas, the soft reed is more flexible, and your lips, which are not yet habituated to this work, can contain it more easily.
> The mouthpiece of the clarinet ought to be put into one's mouth to the two lines near the cut of the reed. Because, if you drive the mouthpiece too far, you will lose the means of control. Similarly, if you don't drive it in enough, you cannot draw a sound. It is necessary then to put it into the mouth like I have said above, to take good care that the teeth touch neither the mouthpiece nor the reed. It is necessary to support the mouthpiece on the lower lip to cover the reed with the upper lip, without the teeth touching any of it. In any case, the teeth ought only to support the lips and give to them the necessary force so to be able to pinch in the higher notes.
> The clarinet ought to be held free and easy. It is unnecessary to advance, or lower, the head because these hinder breathing. It is necessary that the head is correct and unaffected, the left elbow at seven or eight inches from the body, the right elbow elevated a little more, in order that

the instrument falls perpendicularly. It is necessary that the fingers are spread over the holes, the two wrists a little bent, in order that the fingers plug up the holes easily, the thumb of the left hand on the hole and always prepared to take the key and recover the hole. It is necessary when one or several fingers are raised, that they remain perpendicular above the holes which they ought to re-plug, because if one withdraws, one will have too much trouble refinding the holes.[186]

Although Vanderhagen's descriptions are slightly different in wording and amount of detail, the overall presentation of information in his first, second, and third articles remains unchanged from his treatise to that of Blasius:

First Article (and most essential): Positioning the Arms and the Head

This article is very interesting for beginners, as much for acquiring grace in playing as for avoiding the problems that ordinarily result from poor positions. We must then, in carrying the clarinet to the mouth, neither raise nor lower our heads because this impedes breathing freely. We must hold our heads naturally straight without affectation, with the left elbow 5 or 6 inches from the body and the right elbow a little more elevated, so that the bottom of the clarinet is nearly a foot and a half from the body, with the fingers extended on the holes and the two wrists a bit flexible. The holes can now be stopped more easily, for in elevating the wrists and the elbows space is created under the finger and the thumb of the right hand beneath the clarinet, between the first and the second finger. The thumb of the left hand must always be ready to take up the key, or to stop the hole, and consequently must make only very small movements. It is the same for the fingers in general, as we should lift the fingers only a very small distance from the instrument, and always perpendicularly, so that the two hands are always able to lean towards the wood of the clarinet. None of the fingers should touch each other so they can cadence freely. It is also necessary when a finger or several fingers are lifted, that they remain perpendicular above the holes that they must close, for in withdrawing them like many students do, they always have trouble relocating the holes and that impedes execution.

Second Article: On the Embouchure

The embouchure is the basis of all the wind instruments. My object being to discuss that of the clarinet, I will then say that we must not have too much embouchure on the mouthpiece of the clarinet, but only up to the

---

[186] Blasius, 47–48, quoted in Menkin, 65–66.

shoulder of the reed. By extending the clarinet [mouthpiece] too far into the mouth we lose the means of controlling it because it causes pinching which occurs because of a lack of elasticity. The reed is applied on the mouthpiece towards the ligature, and can thus no longer act. We must not then engage the instrument except as I have said previously, by supporting the mouthpiece on the teeth, and covering the reed with the upper lip without the teeth of the upper jaw touching in any circumstance. Because the teeth support and give strength to the upper lip for holding in the high notes, it is also necessary that the sides of the mouth be very firm in order not to allow wind to exit the sides of the embouchure....

Third Article: The Quality of Reeds for Beginners
A beginner must not use a strong reed because it makes the instrument more resistant for him than is effective and because his lips are not yet accustomed to pinching. Strong reeds can also make the clarinet screech and cause it to lose a lot of air through both sides of the mouth. It is necessary then to make a soft reed for the beginner, but not too weak because the sound will resemble a duck....[187]

The differences between these two sections on body posture, reeds, and forming an embouchure could be attributed to Blasius's desire to reduce Vanderhagen's lengthy discussions into brief, succinct statements.

Lefèvre's *Méthode de clarinette*, although it does not reuse any musical examples from either of Vanderhagen's treatises, does seem to have used the 1785 tutor as a template. In *Méthode nouvelle et raisonnée pour la clarinette*, Vanderhagen presents twelve main articles:

First Article: *Positioning the Arms and Head*
Second Article: *On the Embouchure*
Third Article: *The Quality of Reeds for Beginners*
Fourth Article: *Manner of Acquiring a Good Sound*
Fifth Article: *Different Articulations*
Sixth Article: *Triplets or Three-in-One*
Seventh Article: *Appoggiaturas*
Eighth Article: *The Accent*
Ninth Article: *Grace Notes*
Tenth Article: *[Reeds]*
Eleventh Article: *The Trill*

---

[187] Vanderhagen, *Méthode nouvelle et raisonnée pour la clarinette* (1785), 2–3.

Twelfth Article: *Mordents*

Lefèvre presents, among his fourteen main articles, seven on the same topics, and in the same order, as Vanderhagen:

> Article I: *Origin and composition of the clarinet*
> Article II: *The manner of holding the clarinet*
> Article III: *Embouchure and quality of the reed*
> Article IV: *Different notes produced by the same keys*
> Article V: *Position of the lips and fingers*
> Article VI: *Formation of sound*
> Article VII: *Range of the clarinet and distinction of the different sounds it produces*
> Article VIII: *Articulation*
> Article IX: *Ornaments of the melody*
> Article X: *The manner of giving nuance to the sound*
> Article XI: *How to phrase and breathe*
> Article XII: *How to play Adagio*
> Article XIII: *How to play Allegro*
> Article XIV: *The character of the clarinet*

These seven articles discuss the same topics on body posture/positioning, forming an embouchure, reeds, producing a good sound, articulation, and embellishments. Lowell Youngs writes that Vanderhagen's remaining five articles are merely extensions of these main seven:

> Although Vanderhagen presented more than these seven articles, the others are really similar in title as one of the other articles; the article concerning triplets is really a continuation of the discussion of articulation, giving examples of different manners in which triplet patterns may be articulated, and Articles 7, 8, 9, 11, and 12 are all concerned with embellishments.[188]

Such a structural similarity between the two treatises suggests that Lefèvre was familiar with the content and layout of Vanderhagen's 1785 treatise. Lefèvre's

---

[188] Youngs, 118.

Article II: "Manner of Holding the Clarinet and Positioning the Fingers" parallels Vanderhagen's first article, "Positioning the Arms and Head," by commenting, "In order to hold the clarinet with grace and ease, we must hold the head straight and without rigidity, the left elbow placed three or four inches from the body, the right elbow raised nearly an inch and the bell or *pavillon* nearly a foot away from the body."[189] The difference in distance (Vanderhagen said that the left elbow should be five or six inches away from the body) could be attributed to physical differences between the men and their instruments. Lefèvre also reflects his predecessor by reminding the student that proper finger placement will result in excellent technique, although he departs from Vanderhagen by presenting a lengthy explanation of how and where each finger should be placed on the instrument.

Both authors maintain similar stances on forming an embouchure by advocating playing with the reed against the upper lip. Lefèvre advises students to avoid using either too much mouthpiece or placing their teeth on the mouthpiece, and he describes how to gauge one's embouchure based on the structure of the mouthpiece. Vanderhagen makes these same points, although his mouthpiece description differs from that of Lefèvre because mouthpieces at that time could vary widely in terms of width, thickness, and length.

The subject of selecting good reeds occurs twice in Vanderhagen's 1785 treatise in the third and tenth articles. Lefèvre discusses reeds in his third article, although unlike Vanderhagen, who writes separate articles for beginners and advanced players, Lefèvre's comments are clearly directed towards a novice. All three articles emphasize that weak reeds must be avoided because they produce unpleasant sounds, while hard reeds can cause the instrument to squeak and create embouchure fatigue. Both comment that reeds should be examined closely so those that are well dried with medium-sized pores can be selected for use.

---

[189] "Pour tenir la clarinette avec grace et facilité, il faut que la tête soit droite et sans roideur, le coude gauche placé à trios ou quatre pouces du corps, le coude droit plus élevé d'environ un pouce et la patte ou le pavillon à peu pres à un pied de distance du corps" (Lefèvre, *Méthode de clarinette* [1802], 2).

Vanderhagen instructs the student to shave down reeds that are extremely hard and to "break in" all reeds before using them on a regular basis. One discrepancy between authors is that Lefèvre writes that air leaking out of the sides of the mouth results from reeds that are too hard, while Vanderhagen maintains that this is a product of an improper embouchure.

The articles on acquiring a good sound are different between the two treatises. Lefèvre writes that sound production is the result of proper air support, a concept "demonstrated by doctors."[190] He also remarks that the relationship of air support to sound is the same as proper bowing is to the quality of sound on the violin. Vanderhagen describes a good sound as being the result of full air support but he does not mention the physiological elements of air support, nor does he compare it to bowing (articulation is compared to bowing in his fifth article) Students can produce a proper sound by playing slowly and using crescendos and decrescendos so that they can learn to control their air and technique simultaneously. Vanderhagen's musical example for the fourth article in his 1785 treatise is similar to Lefèvre's musical examples in his seventh article on the range and sound characteristics of the clarinet, in that these examples all use dynamic swells to help with embouchure control and sound formation.

The articles on articulation in both treatises reflect the challenges created by playing with the reed on top of the mouthpiece. Vanderhagen and Lefèvre both compare articulation to bow strokes on the violin and add that different articulations are produced through varying strokes of the tongue upon the reed. Lefèvre provides a brief description of how to use the tongue for articulation while Vanderhagen mentions chest articulation. Syllables for articulation are also somewhat similar; Vanderhagen recommends "D" and "T" (he uses "tu" and "te" in his 1799 treatise) while Lefèvre uses "tu." Numerous examples of various articulation exercises are then presented in both treatises, although Vanderhagen repeats much of this information in his sixth article on triplets.

---

[190] "C'est aux physicians à demontrer les causes qui..." (Lefèvre, 8).

Embellishments, although covered by Lefèvre in a single section, comprise five separate articles on appoggiaturas, accents, grace notes, trills, and mordents in Vanderhagen's 1785 treatise. These articles are later combined in his 1799 treatise to create two passages on appoggiaturas and other grace notes, and trills and turns. The only ornament that is not presented in an identical fashion between these methods is the trill, as Lefèvre demonstrates in his musical examples that the trill should begin on the upper note, while Vanderhagen's examples describe how trills can begin on either the upper auxiliary or main note.

The subject of breathing is a topic that is held in common between Lefèvre and Vanderhagen's 1799 treatise. Both authors share the strongly held opinion that improper breathing destroys musical phrases and that breaths must be taken so as to not disrupt phrasing. Breaths may also be taken by shortening a note at the end of a phrase or a cadential point, but this type of breath must not affect the notes that follow it.

Although there are some similarities between the treatises of Vanderhagen, Blasius, and Lefèvre, the quality and presentation of information presented by each author varies. Vanderhagen's 1785 treatise, although relatively brief, offers succinct and logical explanations of many basic elements of clarinet pedagogy, such as body posture and forming an embouchure. His 1799 treatise, in addition to repeating and elaborating upon the material of the 1785 method, provides explanations of the basics of reading and playing music. Although the 1785 treatise seems to have been written for a musically educated audience and the 1799 treatise for beginners, both contain advice, examples, and studies that remain relevant today. This quality of instruction appears to have made an impact on Lefèvre, who used much of Vanderhagen's 1785 work as a template for his 1802 method. Lefèvre relied a great deal on Vanderhagen's earlier *Méthodes* in writing his own similar but original tutor. Blasius's treatise, by comparison, does not contain either the quality or quantity of pedagogical information presented by Vanderhagen in either of his publications. Most of Blasius's writing concerns teaching the basics of reading music, and his discussions of clarinet pedagogy such as body posture, embouchure, reeds, and articulation are given in brief, unimaginative paragraphs. While Blasius imitated several of Vanderhagen's musical examples, he did not use those treatises as exemplars for his own, except perhaps in the hope of having the same success as Vanderhagen.

Chapter 6
The Legacy of Amand Vanderhagen

These translations of Vanderhagen's two Classical instructional treatises on the clarinet have demonstrated the depth and remarkably forward-thinking qualities of his clarinet pedagogy. Their subsequent comparison to treatises by Blasius and Lefèvre have revealed that Vanderhagen's writings provided the basis and inspiration for both of their methods. Biographical information was also gathered to provide a better sense of the musical context in which Vanderhagen worked as a performer and teacher.

Vanderhagen's influence on the development of the clarinet began with his first treatise in 1785, *Méthode nouvelle et raisonnée pour la clarinette*. This was not only the first instructional publication to focus solely on the clarinet, but the first instructional treatise of any kind to discuss in detail pedagogical concepts such as forming an embouchure, body posture, breathing, articulation, and reeds. This information was then expanded upon his second work, *Nouvelle méthode de clarinette* (1799). Although both treatises discuss clarinet pedagogy in a similar manner, Vanderhagen's first treatise does not contain information on learning how to read music. This indicates that this work was not intended for beginners to music but rather was written for musicians seeking to learn how to play the clarinet.

A comparison of Vanderhagen's treatises to Blasius's *Nouvelle méthode de clarinette* (1796) and Lefèvre's *Méthode de clarinette* (1802) shows varying degrees of similarity. Blasius shares few commonalities with Vanderhagen, as Blasius focuses mostly on teaching the student how to read music through a Socratic dialogue. The only noticeable similarities between these authors can be seen in several of Blasius's musical examples that differ from those of

Vanderhagen by a single word, phrase, or sentence. Lefèvre does seem to display an intimate knowledge of Vanderhagen's treatises through his similar organization and presentation of specific pedagogical concepts such as embouchure and reeds. Although these three methods do not share musical examples and refer to two different clarinets (Lefèvre's six-keyed instrument compared to Vanderhagen's five-keyed) Lefèvre does use Vanderhagen's 1785 treatise as a reference and starting point for his own writing.

Although this study indicates the importance of Vanderhagen to the development of clarinet pedagogy and as the creator of the first method book for any instrument, as witnessed by the translations of his two instructional methods, there are remains a considerable lack of information regarding his life and compositions. The gaps in Vanderhagen's biographical information leave numerous questions regarding his early musical training, daily life in Paris, and complete œuvre, and add to the difficulty of ascertaining his legacy. Unlike Lefèvre, whose career in Paris and as a clarinet professor at the Paris Conservatory, and whose students, can be clearly traced, it is still unknown what position Vanderhagen had with the Conservatory, nor have records of his students and their subsequent careers been found. Although most of his treatises' textual content is too archaic for direct use in teaching clarinet today, Vanderhagen's works have enormous significance to the history of clarinet playing and pedagogy, as well as to the formation of the modern method book.

Appendix One

Vanderhagen's Œuvre

Works in Chronological Order

1^{éme} Suite d'*Amusemens militaries* en harmonie pour 2 cors, 2 clarinettes & 2 bassons, contenant les airs de *la Colonie* & autres, mis en ordre par le sieur Armand VANDERAGEN, musicien du Roi. Prix 6 liv. On donnera la suite de ces airs & on les fera tenir port franc par la poste. Chez le sieur de La Chevardière, rue du Roule (*Announces, affiches et avis divers* 7 March 1776 [supplement, p. 212]).

Journal d'harmonie militaire, contenant un choix d'ariettes extraites des opera-comiques, accomodées pour 2 clarinettes, 2 cors de chasse & 2 bassons par Amand VANDERAGEN, musicien des Gardes-françoises, à l'usage des regimens. Prix 60 liv. Il paroîtra douze recueils... dans le courant. On est en état de délivrer les cinq premiers mois d'avance. Chez le sieur de La Chevardière, rue du Roule (*Announces, affiches et avis divers* 9 January 1777 [p. 41]).

1er Recueil d'airs choisis des *Événemens imprévus* et autres arrangées en duo pour deux clarinettes, par A. V. D. HAGEN, musicien de la Garde du Roi, mis au jour par M. Boüin. A Paris, chez M. Boüin, marchand de musique & de cordes d'instruments, rue S. Honoré, près S. Roch, au gagne-petit; Mlle Castagnery, rue des Prouvaires; M. Blaizot, rue Satory à Versailles; & en province, chez les marchands de musique (*Journal de Paris* 28 May 1778 [p. 591]).

Six Duo concertans pour deux flûtes, par M. Amand VANDERHAGEN, musicien de la Garde Françoise du Roi, mis au jour par M. Baillon, successeur de M. Jolivet, éditeur & marchand de musique de la Reine. Prix 6 liv. A Paris, chez l'Editeur, rue Françoise, près la Comédie italienne, à la muse lyrique, & aux addresses ordinaries (*Gazette de France* 2 February 1779, *Journal de Paris* 4 February 1779 [p. 139], *Announces, affiches et avis divers* 15 March 1779 [p. 589]).

Troisième Recueil d'ariettes choisies dans les opéras comiques, arrangées en duo, pour deux clarinettes, par A. V. D. HAGEN, musicien de la Garde du Roi, mis au jour par M. Boüin. Prix 4 liv. 16 s. A Paris, chez l'éditeur, marchand de musique & de cordes d'instruments, rue S. Honoré, près S. Roch, au Gagne-Petit; Mlle Castagnery, rue des Prouvaires; M. Blaizot, rue Satory, à Versailles. A Lyon, Lille, Bruxelles, Bordeaux, & chez les marchands de musique (*Journal de Paris* 18 and 26 February 1780 [p. 207–208 and 239], *Announces, affiches et avis divers* 7 March 1780 [p. 542], *Mercure de France* 15 April 1780 [p. 142] [sans specification du n° de recueil]).

Six Duos concertans pour deux flûtes; dédiés à M. le Comte d'Esterhasy, brigadier des Armées du Roi, Mestre de camp, par A. VANDERHAGEN, œuvre 2^{éme}, Prix 7 liv. 4 s. [Ces duos ne sont pas d'une grande difficulté quoique l'auteur y ait placé quelquefois des traits fort propres à arrêter les commençans & à les exercer par là, d'une manière profitable (*Announces, affiches et avis divers*)]. A Paris, chez Baillon, successeur de M. Jolivet, M^d de musique de la Reine, rue Françoise près de la Comédie italienne, à la Muse lyrique (*Journal de Paris* 5 April 1780, *Gazette de France* 11 April 1780 [p. 142], *Journal de la Librairie* 22 April 1780, *Announces, affiches et avis divers* 27 April 1780 [p. 974]).

Recueil d'airs des ballets en rondeau, tires des meilleurs opéras arrangés pour 2 flûtes concertantes par M. Amand VANDERHAGEN. Prix 3 liv 12 s. Chez M. Mussard, editeurs rue Aubri-boucher, maison d'un marchand de vin; & aux addresses ordinaries (*Journal de Paris* 23 January 1781, *Announces, affiches et avis divers* 26 January 1781 [p. 204]).

Ouverture d'*Iphigénie en Aulide* et Carillon des *Trois Fermiers* en harmonie pour deux clarinettes, deux cors et deux bassons par Amand VAN DER HAGEN. A Paris, chez de La Chevardière, rue du Roule (*Journal de Paris* 11 September 1781).

5^{éme} et 6^{éme} Recueil de petits airs arrangés en duos pour 2 clarinettes par M. Amand VANDER HAGEN. Prix 36 s. Chez Mlle Girard, rue du Roule; & chez tous les m^{ds} de musique de Province (*Gazette de France* 21 December 1781, *Announces, affiches et avis divers* 24 December 1781 [p. 2951] [6^{éme} recueil], *Journal de Paris* 31 December 1781, *Mercure de France* 19 January 1782 [p. 142]).

6 Duos concertans pour 2 flûtes par Amand VANDERHAGEN, musicien de la garde Françoise. Œuvre III. Prix 7 liv. 4 s. Chez Baillon, rue Françoise (*Announces, affiches et avis divers* 14 March 1782 [p. 598], *Gazette de France* 15 March 1782, *Mercure de France* 13 April 1782 [p. 93]).

251

Recueil d'airs tires des meilleurs opéras & opéras-comiques, arrangés pour 2 clarinettes par M. Amand VANDER HAGEN. N°s 7, 8, 9 & 10. Prix 1 liv 16 s chaque. [Chez Melle Girard, rue de la Monnoie] (*Announces, affiches et avis divers* 25 March 1782 [p. 703]).

Recueil d'airs à 2 flûtes, pris dans les opéras d'*Echo & Narcisse*, de *Colinette à la cour* [GRÉTRY], de *Thésée* & autres, arrangés par Armand VANDERHAGEN. Prix 4 liv. 16 s. Chez Baillon, rue Françoise (*Journal de Paris* 30 August 1782, *Announces, affiches et avis divers* 22 September 1782 [p. 2207]).

Airs de *Félix* [MONSIGNY] et suite d'airs de *Colinette à la cour* [GRÉTY] arrangés pour deux flûtes par Amand VAN DER HAGEN. A Paris, chez Baillon, rue Françoise (*Announces, affiches et avis divers* 2 February 1783, *Gazette de France* 7 February 1783, *Journal de Paris* 8 February 1783).

Airs de *Colinette à la cour* [GRÉTY] et de *Félix* [MONSIGNY] arrangés pour en quatours pour deux violins, alto et violoncelle obliges par Amand VAN DER HAGEN. A Paris, chez Baillon, rue Françoise (*Gazette de France* 14 March 1783, *Journal de Paris* 24 March 1783, *Announces, affiches et avis divers* 31 March 1783, *Journal de la Librairie* 5 April 1783).

6 Duos concertans pour 2 flûtes par Amand VANDERHAGEN, musicien au Régiment des Gardes-Françoises, dédiés à Mme de Kerdavy. Œuvre IV. Prix 7 liv. 4 s. Chez Baillon, rue neuve des Petits-champs (*Journal de Paris* 28 November 1783, *Journal de la Librairie* 6 December 1783, *Announces, affiches et avis divers* 9 December 1783 (p. 2939), *Mercure de France* 17 January 1784 [p. 144]).

6 Duos concertans pour deux clarinettes par M. Amand VANDER HAGEN, musicien au Régiment des Gardes-Françoises. Œuvre IV. A Paris, chez de La Chevardière, rue du Roule (*Journal de Paris* 13 March 1784, *Journal de la Librairie* 20 March 1784).

2de Suite d'airs connus en quatuor pour clarinette, bassoon ou violoncelle, violon et alto par M. VAN DER HAGEN, dédiés au chevalier de Vergennes. A Paris, chez Boyer, rue Neuve des Petits-Champs et chez Mme Le Menu, rue du Roule (*Journal de Paris* 29 April 1784, *Journal de la Librairie* 22 May 1784).

11^{éme} – 13^{éme} Recueils de petits airs arrangés en duos pour 2 clarinettes par M. Amand VANDERHAGEN. Prix 36 s. Chez Chez Melle Girard, rue due Roule; & chez tous les m^{ds} de musique de Province (*Journal de Paris* 5 June 1784).

Quatours d'ouvertures et d'airs connus pour flute, violon ou deux violons, alto et violoncelle par M. Amand VANDERHAGEN. A Paris, chez de Roullède, rue Saint-Honoré et chez Mlle Castagnery, rue des Prouvaires (*Journal de Paris* 13 December 1784).

Méthode nouvelle & raisonnée pour la clarinette, où l'on donne une explication Claire & Succinte de la manière de tenir cet instrument, de son étendue, de son embouchure, de la Qualité des anches que les commençans doivent employer, du vrai son, ducoup de langue, en général de tout ce qui a rapport à la clarinette. Cette méthode renferme aussi quelques leçons où les differens coups de langue sont mis en pratique, douze petits airs & six duos très propres à former les élèves, par M. VAN-DER-HAGEN, musicien des Gardes-françoises. Prix 9 liv. A Paris, chez M. Boyer, ancien café de Foy, rue de Richelieu, & Mme Le Menu, rue du Roule, à la clef d'or (*Gazette de France* 5 April 1785, *Journal de Paris* 21 April 1785, *Mercure de France* 23 April 1785 [p. 191]).

Recueil d'airs en duo choisis dans différens operas et opéras-comiques pour 2 clarinettes. Par M. Amand–VANDERHAGEN. Prix 7 liv 4 s. pour Paris et la province port franc par la poste. Chez Le Dux, rue du Roule (*Announces, affiches et avis divers* 19 June 1785 [p. 1943], *Journal de Paris* 20 July 1785, *Journal de la Librairie* 6 August 1785, *Mercure de France* 13 August 1785).

Suite d'airs d'harmonie, arranges pour 2 clarinettes, 2 cors et 2 bassons par Amand VAN DER HAGEN musicien de la garde franç. du Roi n° 20 et 21. Prix 4 liv. 16 s. chaque franc de port. Chez Le Roy (*Gazette de France* 21 March 1786, *Journal de la Librairie* 1 April 1786, *Announces, affiches et avis divers* 14 April 1786 [p. 967]).

6 duos concertans pour 2 flûtes; dédiés à M. le comte de Vergennes, ...par Amand VADER-HAGEN, musicien de la garde française de S.M. Œuvre 12^{éme} et 5^{éme} livre de duo de flute. Prix 7 liv. 4 s. port franc. Chez Baillon, rue du Petit Reposoir, près de la Place des Victoires (*Journal de la Librairie* 16 June 1787, *Journal de Paris* 25 June 1787, *Gazette de France* 24 July 1787, *Announces, affiches et avis divers* 29 July 1787 [p. 2126]).

N°s 13-15, 17-18, et 21 des Pièces d'harmonie par M. Amand VAN DER HAGEN. A Paris, chez Le Duc, rue du Roule. N°s 13-14: *Journal de Paris* 9 October 1785. Nos 15: *Gazette de France* 14 April 1786, *Journal typographique et bibliographique* 22 April 1786. Nos 17: *Announces, affiches et avis divers* 5 August 1786, *Journal de la Librairie* 12 August 1786, *Mercure de France* 19 August 1786. No 18: *Gazette de France* 13 October 1786, *Announces, affiches et avis divers* 18 October 1786, *Journal de la*

Librairie 21 October 1786, *Mercure de France* 4 November 1786, *Gazette de France* 1 December 1786. No 21: *Announces, affiches et avis divers* 14 April 1787, *Mercure de France* 19 May 1787, *Journal de la Librairie* 16 June 1787.

Airs choisis arranges en trio pour deux flûtes et alto par M. Amand VAN DER HAGEN. A Paris, chez Imbault, rue Saint-Honoré (*Journal de Paris*, 19 May 1789).

Méthode nouvelle & raisonnée pour le hautbois, divisée en deux parties: la 1^{éme} partie contient une explication claire & succinte de la manière de tenir cet instrument, de son étendue de son embouchure, de la qualité des anches que les commençans doivent employer, du vrai son, des coups de langue, & en général de tout ce qui a rapport au hautbois: La 2de partie contient plusieurs petits airs, & 6 duos très propres à former des élèves, par Amand VANDERHAGEN. Prix 10 liv. 4 s. Nota on trouvera à la même adresse, la Méthode de flute, par VAN-DER-HAGEN, celle de clarinette, par le même, & celle de basoon par M. OZI Chez M. Boyer, rue de Richelieu, ancien passage du café de Foy (*Announces, affiches et avis divers* 15 January 1792 [p. 194]).

Ouverture et airs du ballet de *Psyché*, arrangés pour deux clarinettes par A. WANDERHAGEN. Prix 6 liv. Les mêmes arrangés pour deux flûtes par le même auteur. Prix 6 liv. A Paris, chez Imbault, professeur et èditeur de musique, rue Honoré, entre la rue des Poulies et la maison d'Aligre, n° 200 (*Journal de Paris* 26 November 1796 [p. 270]).

Il vient de paraître...chez le cit. Sieber fils: Pour flute, VENDERHAGEN, 17 duo faciles. Chez Sieber fils, rue de la Loi, n° 1245, maison ci-devant de Londres (*Journal typographique et bibliographique* 24 January 1799 [n° XVIII, p. 143]).

Il vient de paraître...chez Sieber fils: VANDERHAGEN, 17 duo faciles, pour clarinette. A Paris, chez Sieber fils, rue de la Loi, n° 1245, maison ci-devant de Londres (*Le Courrier des spectacles, ou Journal des theaters et de literature* 30 January 1799).

Une nouvelle méthode de flute par VANDERHAGEN. A Paris, chez I. Pleyel, rue Neuve-des-Petits-Champs, n° 728, entre les rues Anne et de la Loi (*Journal typographique et bibliographique* 14 January 1799 [n° XVI, p. 128], *Journal typographique et bibliographique* 24 January 1799 [n° XVII and XVIII, p. 143–44], *Journal typographique et bibliographique* 28 February 1799 [n° XX, p. 167–68]).

Nouvelle méthode de clarinette par VANDERHAGEN. A Paris, chez I. Pleyel, rue Neuve-des-Petits-Champs, n° 728, entre les rues Anne et de la Loi (*Journal typographique et bibliographique* 29 April 1799 [n° XXVIII, p. 224], *Journal typographique et bibliographique* 4 May 1799 [n° XXIX, p. 232], *Journal typographique et bibliographique* 14 May 1799 [n° XXX, p. 40]).

Pour la flute: VANDERHAGEN, 24 petits Duos [Op. 24?]. A Paris, chez J. Pleyel, éditeur et marchande de musique, rue Neuve-des-Petits-Champs, n° 728, entre les rues de la Loi et celle d'Helvetius (*Journal typographique et bibliographique* 11 December 1799 [n° X, p. 80]).

Pour la clarinette: VANDERHAGEN, 24 Duos faciles [Op. 25?]. A Paris, chez J. Pleyel, éditeur et marchande de musique, rue Neuve-des-Petits-Champs, n° 728, entre les rues de la Loi et celle d'Helvetius (*Journal typographique et bibliographique* 11 December 1799 [n° X, p. 80]).

Pour la clarinette: VANDERHAGEN, 6 Duos faciles. A Paris, chez J. Pleyel, éditeur et marchande de musique, rue Neuve-des-Petits-Champs, n° 728, entre les rues de la Loi et celle d'Helvetius (*Journal typographique et bibliographique* 11 December 1799 [n° X, p. 80]).

Ouverture d'*Epicure* [MÉHUL and CHERUBINI], arrangée pour deux clarinettes, par VANDERHAGEN. Prix 1 fr. 50c. Paris, Pleyel, rue Neuve des Petits-Champs n° 728, entre les rues de la loi et Helvétius (*Journal de Paris* 9 September 1800 [p. 1767]).

Works Without Journal Citations

2e Suite des Amusements militaries contenant un choix d'ariettes tirées des opéra comiques mises en harmonie pour deux clarinettes, deux cors, et deux bassons obliges, en 6 parties. Paris: de la Chevardière, 1776. BnF

4e Suite des Amusements militaires, contenant un choix d'ariettes tirées des opéra comique, mises en harmonie pour deux clarinettes, deux cors et deux bassons obliges, en 6 parties. Paris: de la Chevardière, 1776. BnF

5e Suite des Amusements militaires, contenant un choix d'ariettes tirées des opéra comique, mises en harmonie pour deux clarinettes, deux cors et deux bassons obliges, en 6 parties. Paris: de la Chevardière, 1776. BnF

Pièces d'harmonie contenant des ouvertures, airs et ariettes d'opéra et opéra comiques. Arrangés pour deux clarinettes, deux cors et deux bassons, en 6 parties. Paris: Le Duc, 1787. BnF

Six Duos concertants pour clarinette et bassoon (Oeuvre XIII). Paris: Sieber, 1788. BnF

An Invocation to Friendship, for large choir and orchestra, 1792–1800?

Overture et airs du ballet de Pâris arrangés pour deux clarinettes. Paris: Imbault, 1797. BnF

Overture et airs du ballet de Pâris arrangés pour deux flûtes. Paris: Imbault, 1797. BnF

Pot pourri pour huit instrumens à vent, en 7 parties. Paris: Imbault, 1797. BnF

Six Duos pour deux clarinettes. 10e livre de duos de clarinette. Paris: Imbault, 1797. BnF

Premier Concerto pour flute. Paris: Le Duc, 1800. BnF

Second concerto pour flute. Paris: Le Duc, 1800. BnF

Six morceaux concertants, duetts, de différens auteurs, arrangé pour deux flûtes, et d'une exécution facile, suivis de quatre Etudes faisant suite à la Nouvelle méthode d'Amand Vanderhagen. London: G. Walker, 1800. BnF

Nouvelle methode de flute, divisee en 2 pt. Contenant tous les principes...gravee par les Cnes Marie (28 Dec. 1798). ISSUED SEPERATELY: Les Principes (1817) & Lecons pour l'execution (p. 69) in 1817

Nouvelle methode de clarinette – gravee par les Cnes Marie. ISSUED SEPERATELY: pp.1-73 [Les Principes et les lecons] & pp.74–125 [Airs et duos tires de la methode], 1799.

1e Pot pourri pour deux clarinettes. Paris: Imbault, 1800. BnF

2e Pot pourri pour deux clarinettes. Paris: Imbault, 1800. BnF

Une Folie, ouverture arr. [MEHUL] 1802/3

Une Folie, airs arr. [MEHUL]. 1803 (written for wind band).

Fanfares (or Divertissement militaire) a 4 trp & timb non obl. 1802/3 (1-2)
Picaros et Diego, airs arr [DALAYRAC], 1803– written for winds [wind band]

Le Jeune prude, airs arr. [DALAYRAC] 1806/3

Le Jeune prude, ouverture arr. [DALAYRAC] 1806/3

Le Mariage de Figaro, ouverture arr [MOZART] 1806/4

6 trios arr...2 fl and alto ou fl vl alto [I. PLEYEL] 1806

6 trios d'une difficulte progressive, fl clar bsn [I. PLEYEL], 1808–1815

La naissance du roi de Rome: symphonie militaire à grand orchestre. Paris: Imbault, 1811–12.

Le Grand deuil, airs arr. [BERTON] 1812

Le Grand deuil, ouverture arr. [BERTON] 1812

4 etudes avec les preludes pour une flute, faisant suite a la nouvelle methode. Cap-t: Preludes in all the major and minor Keys. Paris: Pleyel. 1805–1827.

Suite 1: Morceaux choisis des symphonies, arr. [HAYDN], 1817; Suite 2, 1817

Nouvelle methode pour la clar moderne a 12 cles...suivie de tous les principes de musiques...lecons graduees...avec des airs...des duos, des polonaises, des airs varies & plusiers etudes. 19 February 1819.

Airs et duos extr de la methode- 1817; 2nd edition in 1822

Works with No Known Date of Publication

6 duos conc d'une execution facile, 2clar (Bb Eb Bb F g Eb). 14e liv. De duo pour clar. Op.34

Six trios for two flutes and alto

Two suites of *pas redoublés* idem; Paris, Leduc

Three suites of airs from Italian operas for two clarinets, two horns and two bassoons; ibid

Seventeen sets of duos for two clarinets, Paris, at all publishers

3ᵉ concerto, clar princ (Bb). Cap-t: IIᵉ concerto.

Concertos arr en duos [MICHEL]

Concertos for the clarinet, numbers 1, 2, 3, ibid. (Paris, Sieber, Pleyel, P. Petit)

La Création, airs arr. [HAYDN] for wind band

Don Juan, ouverture arr. [MOZART]

Grand military symphony; ibid.

A great military symphony concertante for clarinet, flute, horn, bassoon, and violin obligato

A great military symphony for twelve wind instruments

Lettres à Emilie sur la Mythologie

Pot-pourri in 8 parts; Paris, Janet

Romance of Estelle

Romance of Gonzalve of Cordoue

Vingtquatre petits duos d'une exécution facile pour deux clarinettes Paris, Chez Pleyel.

Wind suites for military band in 10 parts, Op.14, 17, 20, and 21; Paris, Frère

Appendix Two

Works by Amand Vanderhagen Currently In Print

100 Studies for the Clarinet. Edited by Gunther Joppig and Stephen Trier. Wien, Germany: Universal Edition A. G., 1987.

Méthode nouvelle et raisonnée pour hautbois (1792), reprinted in *Hautbois: Méthodes et Traites, Dictionaires.* Edited by Philippe Lescat and Jean Saint-Arroman. Courlay, France: Editions J. M. Fuzeau, 1999.

Méthode pour la flute travesière (n.d.; reprinted in *Tre Metodi per flauto del neoclassicismo francese.* Edited by Marcello Castellani. Firenze: Studio per edizioni scelte, 1984.

Nouvelle méthode de flute. Paris: Chez Pleyel, 1798.

Premier concerto pour clarinette. Hamburg: Musikverlag H. Sikorski, 1961.

Principes pour la clarinette: suivis de quelques airs en duo à l'usage de cet instrument. Paris: De la Chevardiere, 1780.

Quatre etudes avec les preludes: pour une Flûte: faisant suite a la nouvelle méthode. Paris: Chez Pleyel, 1805–27?.

Six duos concertans pour deux clarinettes, 2nd ed. Rotterdam: L. Plattner, 1830–39?.

Six Duos for Two Clarinets (n.d.). Edited by János Malina. Budapest: Editio Musica, 1987.

Tres metodi per flauto del neoclassicismo francese. Firenze: Studio per edizioni scelte, 1984.

Troisieme concerto pour clarinette principale. Rome: Boccaccini & Spada, 2002.

Vingtquatre petits duos d'une execution facile pour deux clarinettes. Paris: Chez Pleyel, n.d..; reprint: Amsterdam: H. C. Steup, 1970.

Appendix Three

Listing of Content for the Methods of Vanderhagen, Blasius, and Lefèvre

Vanderhagen: *Méthode nouvelle et raisonnée pour la clarinette* (1785)

First Article: *Positioning the Arms and Head*
Second Article: *On the Embouchure*
Third Article: *The Quality of Reeds for Beginners*
Fourth Article: *Manner of Acquiring a Good Sound*
Fifth Article: *Different Articulations*
Sixth Article: *Triplets or Three-in-One*
Seventh Article: *Appoggiaturas*
Eighth Article: *The Accent*
Ninth Article: *Grace Notes*
Tenth Article: *[Reeds]*
Eleventh Article: *The Trill*
Twelfth Article: *Mordents*

Vanderhagen: *Nouvelle méthode de clarinette* (1799)

Observation of the Author on this Second Publication
Natural Scale-Explanation of the Scale
Scale on the Sharps and Flats
Advice for Beginners
On the Position of the Body, the Arms, and the Head–A Preliminary Observation
Embouchure
The First Lesson on the Instrument–An Observation
Principles of Music on the Knowledge of Notes
Different Scales
Connected Steps
First Article: *Concerning All the Signs of Which Music is Composed*
Second Article: *Of the Value and the Shape of Notes*
Third Article: *[Dotted Notes and Rests]*
Fourth Article: *[Sharps and Flats]*
Fifth Article: *Sequence of the Signs*

Sixth Article: *On the Number of Sharps Which Are Necessary in Each Key, and to Relative Keys*
Seventh Article: *On the Scale*
Eighth Article: *What the Intervals are Composed of*
Ninth Article: *Instruction on What All of the Inverted Intervals of Minor and Major, and the Augmented and Diminished Intervals, Become*
Tenth Article: *Definitions of Italian Terms That Are Used for Indicating Movements and Nuances*
Eleventh Article: *The Measure*
Twelfth Article: *On Breathing*
Thirteenth Article: *Of Articulations and of the Slur*
Fourteenth Article: *Of Appoggiaturas and Other Grace Notes*
Fifteenth Article: *The Trill and the Turn*
Sixteenth Article: *Lessons on Rests*
Seventeenth Article: *On Syncopation*

Blasius: *Nouvelle méthode de clarinette et raisonnement des instruments* **(1796)**

Explanations of the Principles of Music
First Article: Clef Signs
Second Article: The Staff and Names of Lines and Spaces
Third Article: Note Names
Fourth Article: Accidentals; Major and Minor; Flats
Fifth Article: Sharps
Sixth Article: Note Values
Seventh Article: Measures
Eighth Article: Rests
Ninth Article: Dots; 6/8, 12/8, and 3/8
Tenth Article: Major and Minor Intervals
Eleventh Article: Minor, Diminished, and Augmented Intervals
Twelfth Article: Scales and Orchestration

Lefèvre: *Méthode de clarinette* **(1802)**

Article I: *Origin and composition of the clarinet*
Article II: *The manner of holding the clarinet*
Article III: *Embouchure and quality of the reed*
Article IV: *Different notes produced by the same keys*
Article V: *Position of the lips and fingers*
Article VI: *Formation of sound*
Article VII: *Range of the clarinet and distinction of the different sounds it produces*
Article VIII: *Articulation*

Article IX: *Ornaments of the melody*
Article X: *The manner of giving nuance to the sound*
Article XI: *How to phrase and breathe*
Article XII: *How to play Adagio*
Article XIII: *How to play Allegro*
Article XIV: *The character of the clarinet*

Bibliography

Abraham. *Principes de Clarinette Suivis de Pas rèdoubles et de 7 Marches les Plus a la Mode*. Paris: Frere, 1782.
Baines, Anthony. *Woodwind Instruments and Their History*, 3rd ed. London: Faber and Faber, 1967.
Benoit, Marcelle, ed. *Dictionnaire de la musique en France aux XVIIe et XVIIIe siècles*. Paris: Fayard, 1992.
Benton, Rita and Jeanne Halley. *Pleyel as Music Publisher*. Stuyvesant, NY: Pendragon Press, 1978.
Dorr, Philippe. *Nouvelle Méthode de Clarinette à 6 et à 13 cles, d'après celle de Vanderhagen*. Paris: Aulagnier, 1832 11.
Birsak, Kurt. *The Clarinet: A Cultural History*. Translated by Gail Schamberger. Buchloe: Druck und Verlag Obermayer, 1994.
Boyd, Malcolm, ed. *Music and the French Revolution*. Cambridge: Cambridge University Press, 1992.
Brenet, Michel. "La Libraire musicale en France de 1653 à 1790 après des reigstres de privilèges." *Sammelbände der Internationalen Musikgesellschaft* 8 (1906–07): 401–66.
_____. *Les concerts en France sous l'ancien régime*. Paris, Fischbacher, 1900.
Brymer, Jack. *The Clarinet*. London: Kahn and Averill, 1976.
Buyens, Koen. "Henri-Jacques De Croes and the Court Chapel of Charles of Lorraine. A Socio-Historical Perspective." *Revue belge de Musicologie* 55 (2001). 165–78.
Castillon Frédéric [Adolphe Maximilian Gustav] de. "Clarinette." *Supplément à l'Encyclopédie, ou Dictionnaire Raisonné des Sciences, des Arts et des Métiers*, vol. II. Amsterdam: M. M. Rey, 1776–77.
Charlton, David. "Classical Clarinet Technique: Documentary Approaches." *Early Music* 16 (1988): 396–406.
Cholka, Lynn Ann. "An International Bibliography of Doctoral Dissertations/Treatises/Essays/Theses/Documents Pertaining to the Clarinet." DMA thesis, Florida State University, 1994.
Choron, Alexandre. *Dictionnaire historique des musiciens, artistes et amateurs, morts ou vivans, qui se sont illustrés et une partie quelconque de la musique et des arts qui y sont relatifs*. Paris: Chimot, 1810.
Corrette, Michel, *Méthode Raisonnée pour apprendre aisément à joüer de la Flûte traversiere Nouvelle édition, revüe corrigée et augmentée de la Game du Haut-bois et de la Clarinette*. Paris: Aux Adresses ordinares de Musique, 1773.

de Brossard, Yolande. *Musiciens de Paris 1535–1792*. Paris: Éditions A. and J. Picard, 1965.
de Meude-Monpas, J. J. O. *Dictionnaire de Musique*. Paris: 1787. Reprint, Genève: Minkoff Reprints, 1981.
Dalayrac, Nicolas. *Le Corsaire*. Libretto by Lachabeaussiére. Paris: Leduc, 1783.
Desaugier, M. A. *Les Deux Jumeaux de Bergamo*. Libretto by Florian. Paris: n.p., 1782.
Devienne, François. *Nouvelle méthode théorique et pratique pour la flute*. Paris, 1794.
Devriès, Anik and François Lesure. *Dictionnaire des éditeurs de musique français*, 2 vols. Geneva: Éditions Minkoff, 1979.
Dezède, Nicolas. *Blaise et Babet, ou La suite des trois fermiers*. Libretto by Jacques Marie Boutet de Monvel. Paris: Houbault, 1783.
Drushler, Paul. *The Clarinet: Its Evolution, Literature and Artists*, rev. ed. Rochester, N.Y.: Shall-u-mo Publications, 1979.
Escudier, Léon. *Dictionnaire de musique d'après les théoriciens, historiens et critiques les plus célèbres qui ont écrit sur la musique*. Paris, Bureau central de musique, 1844.
Estock, Joseph James. "A Biographical Dictionary of Clarinetists Born Before 1800." Ph.D. diss., University of Iowa, 1972.
Fétis, François-Joseph. *Biographie universelle des musiciens et bibliographie générale de la musique*, 2nd ed., 8 vols. Paris: Didot Freres, 1860–65. Translated by Jo Rees-Davies. Brighton, England: Top Flat, 1988.
Framery, Nicolas E. and P. L. Ginguené, eds. *Art du Faiseur d'Instruments de Musique et Lutherie extrait de L'Encyclopédie Methodique: Arts et Metiers Mechaniques*, 2 vols. Paris: Panckoucke, 1791–1818, vol. 175–76. Reprint, Geneva: Minkoff, 1972.
Gabucci, Agostino. *Origin and History of the Clarinet*, 3rd rev.ed. Translated by Frederic Lubrani. Memphis: Memphis State University, 1969.
Glick, David Alan. "The Five-Keyed Clarinet." DMA thesis, Eastman School of Music, 1978.
Gradenwitz, Peter. "The Beginnings of Clarinet Literature." *Music and Letters* 17 (1936): 145–50.
Grétry, A. E. M. *L'Embarras des Richesses*. Libretto by Lourdet de Santerre. Paris: P. de Lormel, 1782.
Guy, Larry. *The Daniel Bonade Workbook*. Stony Point, NY: Rivernote Press, 2004.
Hoeprich, T. Eric. "Clarinet Reed Position in the 18th Century." *Early Music* 12 (1984): 49–55.
Hopkinson, Cecil. *A Dictionary of Parisian Music Publishers, 1700–1950*. London: n.p., 1954.
Hotteterre, Jacques. *Méthode pour apprendre à jouer en trés peu de tems de la flûte traversière et des tablatures de la clarinette*. Paris: Bailleux, 1765.
L'Intermédiaire des chercheurs et curieux. Paris: Imp. Centrale Ouest, 1955.

Johansson, Cari. *French Music Publishers' Catalogues of the Second Half of the Eighteenth Century*, 2 vols. Stockholm: Almquist & Wiksells, 1955.

Karp, Cary. "The Early History of the Clarinet and Chalumeau." *Early Music* 14 (1986): 545–51.

Kroll, Oscar. *The Clarinet*. Translated by Hilda Morris. Edited by Anthony Baines. New York: Taplinger Publishing Company, 1968.

Lamneck, Esther. "A Survey of the Music for Two Clarinets, Published ca. 1780–1825, by the Clarinetist-Composers Blasius, Lefèvre, Michel, and Vanderhagen." DMA thesis, The Julliard School, 1980.

Lavoix, Henri. *Histoire de l'instrumentation depuis le seizième siècle jusqu' à nos jours*. Paris, Firmin-Didot et Cie, 1878.

Lawson, Colin. *The Cambridge Companion to the Clarinet*. Cambridge: Cambridge University Press, 1995.

_____. *The Early Clarinet: A Practical Guide*. Cambridge: Cambridge University Press, 2003.

_____. "The Early Clarinet in Theory and Practice." *Journal of the National Early Music Association* 5, no. 2 (Fall 1995): 6–9.

_____. "Playing Early Clarinets: The Lure of History and the Myth of Authenticity." *Musical Performance* 3, no.1 (2001): 23–29.

Lawson, Colin, and Robin Stowell. *The Historical Performance of Music: An Introduction*. Cambridge: Cambridge University Press, 1999.

Le Bihan, Alain. *Francs-Maçons Parisiens du Grand Orient de France*. Paris: Bibliotèque nationale, 1966.

Lefèvre, Jean Xavier. *Méthode de clarinette*. Paris: 1802. Reprint, Genéve: Minkoff Reprints, 1974.

Les Amours D'Été. Libretto by Piis U. Barré. Paris: Vente, 1781.

Lescat, Philippe. *Méthodes et Traités Musicaux en France 1660–1800*. Paris: La Villette, 1991.

Lescat, Philippe, and Jean Saint-Arroman, eds. *Clarinette: Méthodes et Traités, Dictionnaires*. Courlay, France: Éditions J. M. Fuzeau, 2000.

Mather, Betty Bang. *Interpretation of French Music from 1675 to 1775 for Woodwind and Other Performers*. New York: McGinnis and Marx, 1973.

Mather, Betty Bang and David Lasocki. *The Art of Preluding 1700–1830*. New York: McGinnis and Marx Music Publishers, 1984.

_____. *Free Ornamentation in Woodwind Music 1700–1775*. New York: McGinnis and Marx Music Publishers, 1976.

Menkin, William. "Frederic Blasius: *Nouvelle Méthode de Clarinette et Raisonnement des Instruments*: A Complete Translation and Analysis with a Historical and Biographical Background of the Composer and his Compositions for Clarinet." DMA thesis, Stanford University, 1980.

Messenger, Joseph Charles. "An Annotated Bibliography of Selected Books and Periodical Material About the History, Repertoire, and Acoustics of the Clarinet." DMA thesis, University of Iowa, 1971.

Michaud, Louis Gabriel. *Biographie universelle ancienne et moderne.* Paris, Madame C. Desplaces, 1854.

Moore, H. E. and H. Rodney Bennett. *La France Qui Chante: Airs et Paroles Recueillis Ou Choisis.* Boston: D. C. Heath and Company, 1924.

Neumann, Frederick. *Performance Practices of the Seventeenth and Eighteenth Centuries.* New York: Schirmer Books, 1993.

Pierre, Constant. B. *Sarrette et les origines du Conservatoire national de musique et de declamation.* Paris: Delalain frères, 1895.

Pierreuse, Bernard. *Catalogue général de l'édition musicale en France : livres, méthodes et partitions de musique sérieuse en vente.* Paris: Editions Jobert, 1984.

Pino, David. *The Clarinet and Clarinet Playing.* New York: C. Scribner's Sons, 1980.

Principes de Clarinette Avec la Tablature des Meilleurs M^{tres} pour cet Instrument et plusier Duo pour cet Instrument. Paris: n.p., 1775.

Rendall, F. Geoffrey. *The Clarinet: Some Notes Upon Its Construction and History,* 3rd ed. New York: W. W. Norton and Company, 1971.

Rendall, F. Geoffrey, and Herve Audeon. "Amand Vanderhagen." *Grove Music Online.* Edited by L. Macy (Accessed 25 March 2008), <http://www.grovemusic.com>.

Rice, Albert. *The Baroque Clarinet.* Oxford: Clarendon Press, 1992.

_____. *The Clarinet in the Classical Period.* Oxford: Oxford University Press, 2003.

_____. "Clarinet Reed Position." *Early Music* 12 (1984): 429, 431.

_____. "A History of the Clarinet to 1820." Ph.D. diss., Claremont College, 1987.

_____. "Valentin Roeser's *Essay on the Clarinet* (1764), Background and Commentary." MA thesis, Claremont Graduate School, 1977.

Ridenour, Thomas. *The Educator's Guide to the Clarinet.* Denton, TX: T. Ridenour, 2000.

Ross, David. "A Comprehensive Performance Project in Clarinet Literature with an Organological Study of the Development of the Clarinet in the Eighteenth Century." DMA thesis, University of Iowa, 1985.

Ross, Steven T. *French Military History, 1661-1799: A Guide to the Literature.* New York: Garland Publishers, 1984.

Rousseau, Eugene E. "Clarinet Instructional Materials from 1732 to ca. 1825." Ph.D. diss., North Texas State University, 1962.

Sacchini, Antonio. *Renaud.* Libretto by Jean Joseph Leboeuf. Paris: Théodore Michaelis, 1783. Reprint, New York: Broude Brothers Limited, 1971.

Sainsbury, John S. *A Dictionary of Musicians from the Earliest Times,* vol. 2. London: Sainsbury and Co., 1825. Reprint, New York: Da Capo Press, 1966.

Scott, Maxyne Mathisen. "The Clarinet in France in the Mid-18th Century." *NACWPI Journal* 20, no.1 (Fall 1971): 14–16.

Shackleton, Nicholas. "Clarinet." Grove Music Online. Oxford Music Online. 7 December 2008 <http://www.oxfordmusiconline.com/subscriber/article/grove/music/52768>.

Smith, David Hogan. *Reed Design for Early Woodwinds*. Bloomington: Indiana University Press, 1992.

Stieger, Franz. *Opernlexikon, Teil I: Titelkatalog*, 1. Band A–E. Tutzing, Germany: Hans Schneider, 1975.

Stubbins, William. *The Art of Clarinetistry*. Ann Arbor, MI: Ann Arbor Publishers, 1965.

Swanzy, David Paul. "The Wind Ensemble and Its Music During the French Revolution (1789–1795)." Ph.D. diss., Michigan State University, 1966.

Tablettes de Renommée des Musiciens. Paris, 1785. Reprint, Geneva: Minkoff Reprints, 1971.

Thurston, Frederick John. *Clarinet Technique*. London: Oxford University Press, 1964.

Titus, Robert Austin. "The Solo Music for the Clarinet in the Eighteenth Century." Ph.D. diss., State University of Iowa, 1962.

Vanderhagen, Amand. *Méthode nouvelle et raisonnée pour la clarinette*. Paris: Boyer et Le Menu, 1785. Reprint, *Clarinette: Méthodes et Traités, Dictionnaires*. Edited by Philippe Lescat and Jean Saint-Arroman. Courlay, France: Éditions J. M. Fuzeau, 2000.

_____. *Méthode nouvelle et raisonnée pour hautbois*. Paris: 1792, Reprint, *Hautbois: Méthodes et Traites, Dictionaires*. Edited by. Philippe Lescat and Jean Saint-Arroman. Courlay, France: Editions J. M. Fuzeau, 1999.

_____. *Méthode pour la flute travesière*. n.d., Reprinted in *Tre Metodi per flauto del neoclassicismo francese*. Edited by Marcello Castellani. Firenze: Studio per edizioni scelte, 1984.

_____. *Nouvelle méthode de clarinette*. Paris: Pleyel, 1799, Reprint, *Clarinette: Méthodes et Traités, Dictionnaires*. Edited by Philippe Lescat and Jean Saint-Arroman. Courlay, France: Éditions J. M. Fuzeau, 2000.

_____. *Nouvelle méthode de flute*. Paris: Chez Pleyel, 1798.

_____. *Principes pour la clarinette: suivis de quelques airs en duo à l'usage de cet instrument*. Paris: De la Chevardiere, 1780.

_____. *Quatre etudes avec les preludes: pour une Flüte: faisant suite a la nouvelle méthode*. Paris. Chez Pleyel, 1805–1827?

_____. *Six duos concertans pour deux clarinettes*, 2nd ed. Rotterdam: L. Plattner, 1830–39?

_____. *Six Duos for Two Clarinets*. Edited by Janos Malina. Budapest: Editio Musica, 1987.

_____. *Vingtquatre petits duos d'une execution facile pour deux clarinettes*. Paris: Chez Pleyel, n.d., Reprint, Amsterdam: H. C, Steup, 1970.

_____. *100 Studies for Clarinet*. Edited by Gunther Joppig and Stephen Trier. Wien, Germany: Universal Edition A. G., 1987.

Vernet, Carle. *Uniformes napoléoniens*. Paris, 1815.

Warner, Thomas E. *An Annotated Bibliography of Woodwind Instruction Books, 1600–1830*. Detroit: Information Coordinators, 1967.

Weston, Pamela. *Clarinet Virtuosi of the Past*. London: Robert Hale and Company, 1971.

_____. *More Clarinet Virtuosi of the Past*. London: Halstan and Co., 1977.

_____. *Yesterday's Clarinettists: A Sequel*. Yorkshire, England: Emerson Edition, 2002.

Whitwell, David. *Band Music of the French Revolution*. Tutzing, Germany: Verlegt Bei Hans Schneider, 1979.

Youngs, Lowell V. "Jean Xavier Lefèvre: His Contributions to the Clarinet and Clarinet Playing." DMA thesis, The Catholic University of America, 1970.

Index

Abraham, 9–10; *see also Principes de Clarinette Suivis de Pas rèdoubles et de 7 Marches les Plus a la Mode; see also four-keyed clarinet*
Airs à deux Chalumeaux ou deux Clarinettes, 5–6
Altenburg, J. E., 6; *see also Versuch einer Anleitung zur heroisch-musikalischen Trompeter und Pauker-Kunst*
Antoinette, Marie, 13, 23
Baroque clarinet, 6–9; *see also Roeser*
Berg, Lorents Nicolai, 8; *see also Den første prove for begyndere udi instrumental-kunsten; see also three-keyed clarinet*
Biographie Universelle, 10–11, 21, 25, 27; *see also Fétis*
Blasius, Frédéric, 3, 12, 233–40, 247–48; *see also Nouvelle méthode de clarinette et raisonnement des instruments; see also Grand Orient de France*
Castillon, Frédéric Adolphe Maximilian Gustav de, 9–10; *see also Supplement à L'Encyclopédie; see also four-keyed clarinet*
Cartes de sûreté, 15; *see also Vanderhagen*
Chalumeau, 5–6
Choron, Alexandre, 20, 22, 25; *see also Dictionnaire historique des musiciens, artistes et amateurs, morts ou vivans*
Comte d'Esterhasy, 23
Corelli, Antonio, 11; *see also Maldere*
Corrette, Michel, 9–10, 218; *see also Méthode Raisonnée pour apprendre aisément à joüer de la Flûtte traversiere Nouvelle édition, revûc corigée et augmentée de la Gamme du Haut-bois et de la Clarinette; see also four-keyed clarinet, see also Nouvelle édition, revüe corrigée et augmentée de la gamme de hautbois et de la clarinette*
Das neu-eröffnete Orchester, 6; *see also Mattheson*
Demoustier, Charles-Albert, 23
Denner, Johann Christoph, 5
Devienne, Francois, 218; *see also Nouvelle méthode théorique et pratique pour la flûte*
Diapason général de tous les instruments à vent, 9–10; *see also Francoeur*
Dictionnaire historique des musiciens, artistes et amateurs, morts ou vivans, 20, 22, 25; *see also Choron*
Doppelmayr, J. G., 5; *see also Historische Nachricht von den Nürnbergischen Mathematicis und Künstlern*
L'école de musique de la Garde Nationale, 16

Eglise Saint Sulpice, 15: *see also* Vanderhagen
Eisel, Johann Philipp, 8; *see also Musicus Autodidaktos, oder der sich selbst informirende musicus; see also* three-keyed clarinet
Essai d'instruction à l'usage de ceux qui composent pour la clarinette et le cor, 1–2, 8–9; *see also* Roeser
Fétis, François Joseph, 10–11, 21, 25, 27; *see also Biographie Universelle*
Five-keyed clarinet, 7, 10
Florian, Jean-Pierre Claris de, 22–23
Four-keyed clarinet, 9–10; *see also* Hotteterre; *see also* Francoeur; *see also* Castillon; *see also* Abraham; *see also* Corrette
Francoeur, Louis Joseph, 9–10; *see also Diapason général de tous les instruments à vent; see also* four-keyed clarinet
French Revolution, 12, 14–16, 24
Gabucci, Agostino, 26–27
Gamut for the Clarionet, 8; *see also* three-keyed clarinet
Garde Consulaire, 17
Garde du Directoire, 17
Garde Françoise du Roi, 11–15
Garde Imperiale, 17–19
Garde Nationale, 11–17; *see also* military bands
Grand Orient de France, 11–12; *see also* Blasius; *see also* Vanderhagen; *see also* Yost
Gravier, Charles, 23–24; *see also* Vergennes
Handel, Johann, 7
Hapsburg, Maria Anna of, 10
Haussmann, Baron, 15

Hayden, Joseph, 11; *see also* Maldere
Historische Nachricht von den Nürnbergischen Mathematicis und Künstlern, 5; *see also* Doppelmayr
Hotteterre, Jacques, 9–10; *see also Méthode pour apprendre à jouer en trés peu de tems de la flûte traversière et des tablatures de la clarinette; see also* four-keyed clarinet
Hugray, 19–20
Institut Nationale de Musique, 16; *see also* Paris Conservatory
Jadin, Paul Adrien, 14
Journal of Military Music, 14, 24
Kerdavy, Mme de, 23
Kroll, Oscar, 17
La cathédrale Notre-Dame d'Anvers, 10; *see also* Vanderhagen
Lefèvre, Jean-Xavier, 2, 233–45, 247–48; *see also Méthode de clarinette*
Légion d'Honneur, 18–19; *see also* Napoleon
Lorraine, Prince Charles Alexander of, 10
Majer, Joseph Friedrich, 7–8; *see also Museum Musicum theoretico practicum das ist neu-eröffneter theoretische und practischer Music-Saal*
Maldere, Pierre van, 10–11; *see also* Corelli; *see also* Hayden; *see also* Mozart; *see also* Vanderhagen
Mattheson, J., 6; *see also Das neu-eröffnete Orchester*
Menkin, William, 174
Méthode de clarinette: fingering charts, 235–36; musical examples in, 236–37; structure of, 233–34;

Vanderhagen, similarities to, 240–45, 247–48; *see also* Léfèvre
Méthode nouvelle et raisonnée pour la clarinette: analysis of, 213–21, 230–31; articulations, 37–41; body posture, 33–34; embellishments, 41–44, 45–47; embouchure, 34–35; etudes, 57–90; fingering charts, 32–33; meter, 39–41, 47–52; reeds, 35, 44–45; sound production, 36; translation of, 29–91; transposition, 54–57; trills, 45–46; Yost, dedication to, 91, 221; *see also* Vanderhagen
Méthode pour apprendre à jouer en trés peu de tems de la flûte traversière et des tablatures de la clarinette, 9–10; *see also* Hotteterre
Méthode pour la nouvelle clarinette et clarinette-alto, 2; *see also* Müller
Méthode Raisonnée pour apprendre aisément à joüer de la Flûtte traversiere Nouvelle édition, revûe corigée et augmentée de la Gamme du Haut-bois et de la Clarinette, 218; *see also* Corrette
Military bands, 11–19
Mozart, Wolfgang Amadeus, 11; *see also* Maldere
Müller, Ivan, 2; *see also Méthode pour la nouvelle clarinette et clarinette-alto*
Museum Musicum theoretico practicum das ist neu eröffneter theoretische und practischer Music-Saal, 7–8: *see also* Majer
Musicus Autodidaktos, oder der sich selbst informirende musicus, 8; *see also* Eisel
Napoleon, 17–19, 21–22; *see also Légion d'Honneur*
Nouvelle édition, revüe corrigée et augmentée de la gamme de hautbois et de la clarinette, 218; *see also* Corrette
Nouvelle méthode de clarinette et raisonnement des instruments: fingering charts, 235–36; musical examples in, 236–37; Vanderhagen's writing, imitation of, 237–40, 247–48; structure of, 234–33, *see also* Blasius
Nouvelle méthode pour la clarinette: analysis of, 222–31; articulation, 146–50; author's note, 95; body posture, 99–101; bass pitches, 142–43; beginners, advice to, 99; breathing, 123–25; chromatics, 114, 131; counting, 110–11, 112, 123, 132–42; embellishments, 150–53; embouchure, 101–102; etudes, 144–45; fingering charts, 96–99; music terms, 121–23; preludes, 207–12; principles of music, 102–23, 125–30, 144–45, 154–60; rests, 112, 160–85; shapes of notes, 110–11; syncopation, 185–96; translation of, 93–212; transposition, 201–07; *see also* Vanderhagen
Nouvelle méthode théorique et pratique pour la flute, 218; *see also* Devienne

Paris Commune of 1871, 15, 24
Paris Conservatory, 16–17; *see also Institut Nationale de Musique; see also L'ecole de musique de la Garde Nationale*
Paris *Opéra*, 19–20
Péchignier, Gabriel, 19
Pleyel & Fils aîné, 26
Pleyel and Naderman, 26
Prince of Guémené, 13–14; *see also Rohan, Jules Hercule Meriadec de*
Principes de Clarinette Avec la Tablature des Meilleurs M^{tres} pour cet Instrument et plusier Duo pour cet Instrument, 9–10; *see also* four-keyed clarinet
Roeser, Valentin, 1, 8–9; *see also Essai d'instruction à l'usage de ceux qui composent pour la clarinette et le cor*
Rohan, Jules Hercule Meriadec de, 13–14; *see also* Prince of Guémené
Versuch einer Anleitung zur heroisch-musikalischen Trompeter und Pauker-Kunst, 6; *see also* Altenburg
rue du Dragon, 20; *see also* Vanderhagen
rue Saint Marguerite, 14–16; *see also* Vanderhagen
Sainsbury, John, 20–22, 27
Sarrette, Bernard, 16; *see also Institut Nationale de Musique; see also L'ecole de musique de la Garde Nationale; see also* Paris Conservatory
Tablettes des Renommée, 21–22
The Compleat Tutor for the German Flute, 8

Théâtre Français, 19–20
Three-keyed clarinet, 6–7, 8; *see also* Eisel; *see also* Berg; *see also Gamut for the Clarionet*
Vanderhagen, Amand Jean François Joseph: *cartes de sûreté*, 15; French Revolution, 12, 14–16, 24–25; *Garde Consulaire*, 17; *Garde Françoise du Roi*, 11–15; *Garde du Directoire*, 17; *Garde Imperiale*, 17–19; *Grand Orient de France*, 11–12; *Légion d'Honneur*, 18–19; life in Belgium, 10–11, 15–16; life in Paris, 11–20; *Méthode nouvelle et raisonnée pour la clarinette*, 1, 3, 10, 26, 29–91; method books, 25–27; Napoleon, 17–19, 21–22; *Nouvelle méthode pour la clarinette*, 1, 25–26, 67–158; *Nouvelle méthode pour la clarinette moderne à douze clefs*, 3, 25; Paris Conservatory, 16–17; Paris *Opéra*, 19–20; *Théâtre Français*, 19–20; vocal music, 22–23
Vergennes, M. le comte de, 23–24; *see also* Gravier
Versuch einer Anleitung zur heroisch-musikalischen Trompeter und Pauker-Kunst 6; *see also* Altenburg
Vivaldi, Antonio, 7; *see also* Baroque clarinet
Yost, Michel, 12, 91
Weston, Pamela, 12; *see also* Vanderhagen

Joan Michelle Blazich

Dr. Joan Michelle Blazich holds a Doctorate of Musical Arts in Clarinet Performance from the University of Cincinnati College-Conservatory of Music in Cincinnati, Ohio. Dr. Blazich is an award-winning clarinetist who has performed extensively throughout the United States, Europe, and Russia.